Dr. Paula's House Calls to Your Newborn

Dr. Paula's House Calls to Your Newborn

Paula M. Elbirt, M.D., FAAP
Medical Director, www.drpaula.com

FISHER
BOOKS™

Illustrations by ALICE SIMPSON © 1994, 2000

Library of Congress Cataloging-in-Publication Data

Library of Congress Cataloging-in-Publication Data
Elbirt-Bender, Paula.
    Dr. Paula's house calls to your new baby / by Paula M. Elbirt.
      p. cm.
    Includes bibliographical references and index.
    ISBN 1-55561-293-8 (hardcover : alk. paper) — ISBN 1-55561-255-5
      (pbk. : alk. paper)
    1. Infants (Newborn)—Care. 2. Parenting. I. Title: Doctor Paula's
    house calls to your new baby. II. Title: House calls to your new baby.
    III. Title.
    RJ253.E427 2000
    649'.122—dc21   00-034822

Fisher Books
5225 W. Massingale Road
Tucson, Arizona 85743-8416
(520) 744-6110

Fisher Books is a member of the Perseus Books Group.

Find us on the World Wide Web at http://www.fisherbooks.com

Fisher Books' titles are available at special discounts for bulk purchases in the United States by corporations, institutions, and other organizations.

Text design: Anne Olson
Production: Randy Schultz
Cover design: Lynne Bishop

First printing, September 2000

1 2 3 4 5 6 7 8 9 10—03 02 01 00

Contents

Introduction

More than once in my 18 years of practice as a pediatrician, a mother has called and introduced herself by saying, "Hello, I'm a newborn mother." Of course what she meant to say was, "I'm the mother of a newborn." But there's truth in this slip of the tongue. In what I call *the tenth month*—those weeks after her baby's birth—a woman is reborn into her new role as mother. She is still a wife, friend, daughter, daughter-in-law, but even those roles are changed forever. As one mom said to me, "I'm not who I used to be, but I'm not exactly who I expected to be, either." I tell mothers there is life after childbirth, but it's not the same one. The transformation into the mother role eclipses all of the others, at least for a time.

Not surprisingly, new moms have questions and concerns about caring for their babies. In the first few hours and days, the concerns are fundamental: "Is my baby normal?" "Is she healthy?" Then come all the questions about taking care of the baby, which are asked with incredible predictability. Most new mothers need information on how to deal with the reality and responsibility of the small bundle of joy nestled in their arms.

Moms frequently experience what I have come to call "mother muddle"—a state of neediness and confusion. Nothing quite prepares mothers for this new fact of life: You are now totally responsible for another human being. New mothers need to understand what has happened to them and what will happen to them in the weeks to come.

New mothers also have many questions about caring for themselves. When I do the routine two-week checkup of the baby, I always ask the mother, "How are you?" And they tell me. (As the mother of three children, I understand what they are going through.) Often, after we've met, I get calls from these same mothers with questions not only about their babies, but more commonly, they ask me about concerns they have about themselves as well. ("When I pass the mirror, I don't recognize myself," or "I know I'm supposed to be happy, but all I do is cry," or "I feel so dumb. I thought breastfeeding was supposed to be so easy.") They ask, "Should I be calling you?" and I invariably answer, "Who else would you call?" After an intense nine-month relationship, their obstetrician/gynecologist has often faded from the picture, and the pediatrician is now clearly in the spotlight. You could say that pediatricians really have two "patients": mother and baby. We cannot separate the two. I wouldn't want to.

Use this book along with your naturally good instincts.

Dr. Paula's House Calls to Your Newborn will track the journey both mother and child embark upon after birth through the first six months. Although this book will try to address the myriad questions I have been asked, it should be used along with your naturally good instincts. I tell "my parents," no one knows your baby as well as you do. Use what advice feels right; what doesn't, discard.

Over the years, I have conducted "new-mother's groups"— after-hours sessions just for moms. I began these groups as a "cure" for a common affliction: New mothers are often isolated and alone. Mothers don't just need information. They ache for reassurance—to hear that what they are experiencing is being experienced by other mothers as well. I've tried to gather my mothers together, not in one room, but into this book. Their voices, both their victories and laments, fill *Dr. Paula's House Calls to Your Newborn*.

This book will help promote what I call the *3 Cs*— Competence, Confidence and Comfort. My objective always is to help "raise" happy moms because inevitably only happy moms produce happy babies.

Part I

The Hospital Experience

1

The Newborn Baby

Congratulations! You have finally given birth. After nine months of daydreaming and planning, you have reached that magic moment—a moment that has to be experienced to be understood.

No one can really describe what a newborn baby FEELS like when she emerges into this world. It's miraculous, plain and simple. Don't be surprised if time seems to stand still and images are distorted—but just momentarily.

The Delivery Room Experience

The baby emerges with a final push. In a vaginal delivery, what you see first is a lot of bloody fluid. Very soon afterward your glistening, sparkling, shiny wet baby is slid up and over your pelvis and onto your belly. She is still attached to the winding umbilical cord emerging from between your legs. As she is handed up to you, the cord lengthens along with her.

In a Cesarean section, also called a *C-section*, if you are awake (and the majority of women are), the baby will be lifted into the air still attached to the cord and placed in your arms at your chest. In emergency C-sections, the baby will first be quickly examined and then shown to you when everything is determined to be "okay."

Most mothers are so relieved and dazzled by the baby that they don't pay much attention to the cord or for that matter to most of what is happening at their pelvis.

At the moment of birth, you will hear someone announce the exact time, but you *won't* see a nurse turn the baby upside down and slap her as in old movies.

When the baby's head first appears or just when the baby is put on your stomach, you will probably hear odd "gurgling" noises as the doctors and nurses suction from your baby's mouth and nose the amniotic fluid she swallowed in her passage through the birth canal. (Amniotic fluid is the clear pinkish liquid in which the baby floated while in utero.) Some babies, particularly in vaginal deliveries, need extra suctioning, so you may hear slurping sounds, a lot like a vacuum cleaner makes, as the nurse uses a flexible tube in the baby's mouth to help your baby breathe more easily.

Cutting the Cord

Unless you have prearranged with your obstetrician to have your partner participate in cutting the cord, the doctor will snip and clamp it with a special plastic device. Instead of a clamp, some hospitals use "tripledye," a chemical that dries up the cord. The cord will look like it's been dyed purple.

Once the baby is brought to your chest, you may feel a tugging on your uterus. It may be somewhat painful, but at this moment it seems largely irrelevant when compared to the precious baby in your arms. You may see some of what's going on at your pelvis and feel discomfort or even sharp pain while the placenta (also called the *afterbirth*) is coming out. Your focus once again will still be on your newborn. If the doctor needed to widen the exit from your vagina with a cut, he or she will also be stitching it back up; this is called *episiotomy*.

Babies get cold quickly. The nurses will put little blankets over the baby right away, while she is still connected to you by the umbilical cord.

The Bonding Period

Most parents confide that the newborn looks less than beautiful— actually quite wrinkled and purple—and that is just fine! No other moments rival these first few after a birth. It's special even for the staff in the delivery room. When I was a pediatric resident, I was in the delivery room often, and never saw anyone connected with a birth respond casually to this truly blessed event. This is actually the period researchers referred to when they originally described the need for mothers to bond with their babies. Some babies alternately cry and then calm in your arms. This Is a wonderful opportunity to help the baby to suck on your breast: If you place the newborn at your nipple, she will usually suck, even though there is no milk. (In fact, she may not suck again this calmly until many hours later.)

Some babies alternately cry and then calm in your arms.

This magic time actually lasts for just a few minutes, which is usually long enough. As exhaustion sets in, especially in your arms and legs, a nurse will take your baby just a few feet away and put her on a warmer. This is a specially built infant-sized bed where heat lamps radiate down from the top. A small probe, which doesn't hurt or burn, will be taped to your baby's body to monitor her temperature so that the warmer is always at the correct setting.

Your natural instinct will be to follow the baby. If you turn and look to your side, you may see the nurse cleaning and drying her on the warmer. Then you'll see the nurse listening intently to the baby's chest with a stethoscope, flicking the baby's heels, picking up her arms and letting them drop in what appears to you to be a rather abrupt manner. It's all routine. The nurse is making a determination of your baby's Apgar score.

The Apgar Score

Apgar scores are universally taken at 1 minute, 5 minutes, and in some cases, 10 minutes to evaluate or measure the baby's health in five areas: respiration, heart rate, muscle tone, reflexes and color. The baby isn't put through specific tests but rather is observed and given a 0, 1, or 2 in each area. In the best circumstances, the total score would be 10 (which is where the expression "a perfect 10" originally came from). Rarely if ever can a baby get a 10 at the first minute of life because they are "less than pink" at birth. (Variations in color from slightly pale to rosy are perfectly normal.) Generally speaking you are not told the score, unless you ask, but typically a healthy baby gets at least a 7. C-section babies tend to have slightly higher Apgar scores, because they don't have much difficulty coming out and their color is usually better.

Apgar Table

Sign	Points		
	0	1	2
Appearance (color)*	Pale or blue	Body pink, extremities blue	Pink
Pulse (heartbeat)	Not detectable	Below 100	Over 100
Grimace (reflex irritability)	No response to stimulation	Grimace	Lusty cry
Activity	Flaccid (no or weak activity)	Some movement of extremities	A lot of activity
Respiration (breathing)	None	Slow, irregular	Good (crying)

*In nonwhite children, the color of mucous membranes of the mouth; whites of the eyes; lips; palms; hands; and soles of the feet are examined.

Eye ointment. You will also see the nurse putting ointment in the eyes to protect the baby from a variety of infections that could occur during the birth process. You may also hear the baby cry as she is given a shot of vitamin K in her thigh to prevent a rare cause of bleeding in newborns. In some hospitals, the baby is given a shot of penicillin to prevent a specific type of infection caused by a vaginal bacteria.

Wristbands and ankle bands. In the delivery room, your baby will be registered and a tag put on her ankle. The baby will be footprinted and you will be fingerprinted right onto the birth certificate, so that for all time it's clear that you are this baby's mommy. You will be given a wristband that matches your baby's ankle band.

The need to count fingers and toes . . . is overwhelming.

Examining Your Baby

The nurses will wrap up the baby after the five-minute Apgar and give you back your dried, tested, registered and quite wonderful baby. This is often when I see new mothers peek carefully under the blankets, almost as if they are afraid to mess them up. The need to count fingers and toes and really look at this baby is overwhelming. Both parents will exclaim: "Oh my, he looks just like . . . " or "Who does he look like?"

Parents will joyfully respond when they see what they "like": "Oh, look, he has beautiful blue eyes," and occasionally also be taken aback at what appears to be less than perfect: "What's this bruise, this bump, this red mark?" Most of these birthmarks are just that—the result of the process of birth—and fade away in just a matter of hours. (More about these marks later.)

After you've examined this nicely wrapped baby (who, as a result, may be slightly unwrapped), there will come a time—anywhere from fifteen minutes to an hour and a half later—when the nurses take the baby to the nursery and you to the recovery room. (In some hospitals, the baby will be wheeled with you to the recovery room and then taken to the nursery.) You may feel a little sad to let her go so soon, or you might just be relieved.

For additional information about obstetrics, gynecology, and your pregnancy, visit the drpaula.com Web site at this address:

http://obgyn.drpaula.com

The clerk in the delivery area will call up to the nursery and announce: "Baby coming up!" In more and more hospitals, "rooming in" is commonplace—baby stays in the same room with mother until they go home, if there have been no complications in the birth.

The Nursery

Your baby is now in the nursery—a glass-enclosed room where there is a lot of contact between the staff and the babies. Your baby is the "new kid on the nursery block," which alerts the staff to keep an eye on her. A nurse will completely unwrap the baby and put her on the scale to determine her birth weight. Then she will take your baby's measurements: length and size of head, chest and abdomen. She will be placed once again on a warmer where she will be observed naked for the next two to three hours.

While she is on the warmer, her temperature will again be monitored by a probe, which is attached to her by tape. The nurse will do a full examination of the baby, listening to the heart and making sure the lungs are clear. (I often see the daddy outside the nursery window watching all the goings-on.)

What Is Baby Feeling?

During this period, the baby often appears to be very calm and peaceful. If you could peek in to the nursery you would see her lying very quietly, making some smooth

Babies need time to recover from the birth experience.

movements and occasionally jerky ones— very similar to what she was like in the womb. She may even curl into a fetal position. If you've had anesthesia, the baby has gotten some of it too through the umbilical cord and could be a little groggy. Your baby needs to slowly recover from the experience of childbirth. (I'm often reminded of the "talking" newborn in the movie *Look Who's Talking* who, immediately after birth, keeps repeating: "Put me back!")

Why Is My Baby Swaddled?

It's been observed that babies are usually much happier when they are swaddled—that is, wrapped in snug-fitting clothes and blanket. (Remember your baby has been in pretty tight quarters for the last nine months.) The reason behind swaddling is that babies are subject to the Moro or startle reflex, which causes their limbs to flail out and back at random times (see page 16).

Babies have no control over this neurological event, which momentarily upsets them. It can be somewhat reduced by swaddling. (For instructions on how to swaddle your baby yourself, see page 112.)

After a few hours of observation, the baby will be dressed in hospital clothing. Most hospitals use loosely cuffed T-shirts with strings or snaps, a baby diaper and a little "sock hat" on her head to keep her warm: The head is such a large part of her overall body that a lot of heat can be lost through it. Finally, baby will be wrapped in a square cotton swaddling blanket.

Long fingernails? If baby has long nails, which is the case for many postmature babies (those babies who were born after 40 weeks of gestation), then she will be dressed in a long-sleeved T-shirt with cuffs that can be pulled down over her fingers so that she won't scratch herself. To prevent the accidental nipping of the skin, nurses are instructed to leave the nails unclipped. (See page 133 for how to cut baby's nails once you get home.)

Your baby is almost ready for the journey to your room. She will be put into a crib with a label attached to it listing vital information, such as her last name, your name, time of birth and

For swaddling preemies, click on this helpful Web site:
http://www2.medsch.wisc.edu/childrenshosp/ parents_of_preemies/swaddling.html

birth weight. The nurse keeps track of events as they happen to your baby, such as "first urination" and "first stool," often by recording them on the chart on the crib.

Getting to Know Your Newborn

Once your baby has been brought to your room and the distractions of the delivery room are gone, the two of you have the perfect opportunity to get to know each other. Take a moment to undress your baby completely and just look at her, a new little person in her own right.

Baby's looks. Babies change a great deal the first few days. The baby handed to you on the delivery table may in fact look very little like the one you see now, only a few hours later. Her head may still be very pointy, odd or misshapen, but less so than at birth. A 4-hour-old baby rarely resembles those perfect infants who reside on detergent boxes and baby-formula cans.

If you had a C-section, your baby will look more like what you expect a baby to look like because she hasn't traveled through the vaginal canal. Her face will be less flattened and the head rounder.

A work in progress. I tell all new mothers: Think of your newborn as a work in progress. Babies are unfinished, from their GI (gastrointestinal) tract to the muscular system. Few of the many functions of the body are working at complete capacity yet. There is a lot of fine-tuning ahead, which will develop with usage. For example, the signals from the brain that tell the two eyes to focus together on the same thing aren't coordinated yet, so newborns are often described as "cockeyed." Control of body temperature is uneven, so she may overheat or chill easily. Everything inside your baby is developing in fits and starts. You could say that what you are holding is just a sketch of your baby; the entire picture will be slowly and brightly colored in.

Think of your newborn as a work in progress.

Fetal Position

As you look at your baby, you will notice that her body is still in a fetal position. The newborn maintains this position for many weeks after birth. It serves a purpose: Babies aren't born with the best temperature regulation and this position helps keep the warmth and heat closer to their bodies. Her shoulders are hunched up, her arms are flexed, and her hands are fisted. As her ability to move develops and her body grows, she will gradually unfold out of these positions.

> If your baby was born in a breech position—her buttocks emerged first—you may find her sucking on her toes for a few days. In the womb, her hips were flexed and her knees held high up on her chest.

Your Little Prizefighter

You may notice lots of little marks and blemishes. I like to think of it this way: Your baby is like a little prizefighter. She's survived nine months underwater and then gone "10 rounds" through the birth canal. She's emerged the "winner," with all the bumps and bruises to prove it. She may have a little scab on her head from the fetal monitor. She may have pimples on her body *(erythema toxicum)* as a result of your hormones, and her fingers and toes may be a little purple.

Babies are often accused of looking like little old men. That's because there are a lot of wrinkles and folds all over them as the result of having soaked in an amniotic fluid bath for nine months and then retaining some of that fluid after birth.

Birth-related marks. Your baby may, in fact, have a variety of birth-related marks. At the base of the neck, you may see "stork" bites. These are so named because that is supposedly where the stork carries the baby with its beak! The official name is *nevus flameus*, which simply means "red mark" and is a collection of tiny blood vessels

Some babies are born with "stork bites."

under the skin. They may also be present between the eyebrows, under the nostrils or on the eyelids.

These irregularly shaped marks are flat and have no special texture. There may also be a bluish discoloration at the base of the spine or over the buttocks. No one knows why any of these marks appear, but almost universally all of them fade by the time the baby celebrates her first birthday.

From Head to Toe: Inside and Out

🍋 Some babies are born with a lot of **hair** but most are almost bald at birth. Babies who have dark hair on their heads tend to have body hair as well, which covers their shoulders, the small of their back, maybe the forehead and tips of their ears. Your baby will not grow into a gorilla or transform at night into a tiny werewolf; most of this hair will gradually fall off. The texture of the fine "primary" hair will change, but at first it's scattered unevenly, and may even stick straight up. Even bald babies have some fuzz.

🍋 The **head** makes up about one third of babies' surface area and is almost huge in relation to the rest of their bodies. Babies appear to have large foreheads because they have so little hair.

🍋 Everybody has heard about the "soft spot" or **fontanelle**, but there are actually two soft spots. One is right smack at the top

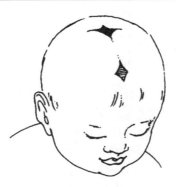

The newborn's head has two small openings called fontanelles.
The smaller posterior fontanelle closes soon after birth. The anterior one,
known as the soft spot, *is open into the second year of life.*

What Is the Fontanelle?

So that the skull can accommodate the baby's brain as it grows, the head is made up of six overlapping flat bones. These bones slide apart as needed to give the growing brain more room.

Run your hand gently over your baby's head and you'll feel many irregularities or ridges. These are all normal. They are the edges of these skull bones as they override each other.

of the head, and the second, smaller one is slightly toward the back. Although perfectly normal, this second one is the cause of some phone calls to me in the middle of the night.

- The **eyes** may cross. Most are a gray, slate color, which will change by six months.
- The **lids** are puffy and don't stay open long.
- The **eyebrows** and **lashes** are faint and not easy to see.
- The **ears** may appear not to match. One may be curled forward and one back.
- The **nose** has a flat, wide bridge.
- The **tongue** may stick out.
- The inside of the **mouth** has ridges and may have several white bumps.
- The **cheeks** are puffy and may be hard.
- The **chin** recedes.
- The **skin** will begin to exfoliate, or flake. It is often driest at the ankles and wrists.
- The **nipples** may be hard and knobby and may even leak a clear fluid.
- The **belly button** has a one- or two-inch long yellowish, plastic-looking stump.

❥ The **hands** and **feet** may be purplish in color.

❥ The **nails** are long, thin, transparent and often quite sharp.

❥ The **genitalia** of babies are enlarged by the pressure on them during a vaginal birth and the large quantity of hormones transferred from the mother.

The vulva and labia in girls and the scrotum in boys all appear quite large in comparison to the rest of the body. Your new daughter may have a vaginal discharge, which is quite normal.

In most boys, when the scrotum is relaxed, you can see and feel two marble-sized testicles. Some boys are born with one or both testicles not yet in the scrotum. Often this condition takes care of itself within a year. The pediatrician should discuss this with you.

The penis has a covering of skin, known as the *foreskin*, which extends over the top of the penis and narrows a bit, a little like a sock that is pulled too long on a foot. If the penis is left uncircumcised, this foreskin will remain. If the baby is circumcised, the foreskin will be removed (see pages 18 and 19).

What Can My Baby Do?

Noted child researcher Dr. Michael Lewis, and his teams, have thousands of hours of tape recordings of new babies. His aim is to document what a baby can do.

Babies are born with a considerable repertoire of skills.

The research clearly indicates that, rather than being a blank slate that needs to be filled in with information, a baby is born with a considerable repertoire of skills. All of her senses are operating—she can smell; taste (babies reject formula they don't like, and although they are toothless, we know they are born with a "sweet tooth"); feel (in fact, they have a highly developed sense of touch and will often soothe when you hold them. And we know they can feel pain); hear; and see.

A Communicating Team

What Lewis and other researchers, such as Dr. Stanley Greenspan, have discovered is that even newborns try to communicate with us. Babies are really half of a communicating team from the moment of birth. Your daughter can "talk" to you if only you know how to translate.

> A newborn can see best at about six to 12 inches away—the rest is fuzzy. She blinks her eyes open and shut as you get closer to her and flutters her eyelids when you withdraw.

Eye contact. For instance, it's been noted that almost from birth, a baby will look to catch your eye. She can't focus on you for long, and she can only see well about a foot or so away; but if you smile when she catches your eye, she will catch your eye for longer periods. You may even be rewarded with a rudimentary smile. It won't be a full-blown grin, of course, but the corners of her mouth will curl up a little bit. (Try it! Smile repeatedly when she looks at you.)

Sounds. Your baby can make sounds. She can make high- and low-pitched cries, but she can't modulate very well. Mostly she makes soft squeaks, tweaks and grunts—sounds that are produced in the voicebox but seem to come from deep within her chest.

Hearing. Baby can hear at birth but she won't always respond to sounds. (Don't test your baby's hearing by clapping your hands around her head; her lack of an immediate response may disappoint or even alarm you.) Babies have the ability to inhibit noises selectively; sometimes they respond, even in their sleep, to soft noises; and sometimes they don't respond to loud ones even when they are awake. They do seem to prefer soft sounds—possibly because for nine months they listened to the world through several layers of your body—and repetitious sounds, perhaps reminiscent of the sound of your heartbeat.

Movements. In terms of motor skills, you will see that your baby can move her arms, kick her feet, cry, blink her eyes, open and close her mouth, suck and grasp—she may even tug on your hair or your finger. She can move her head but she doesn't have strong neck muscle control yet, so she can only lift her head briefly. The head appears to be in a lot of motion as she twists it from side to side. If you put the baby on your shoulder she may stretch out her neck momentarily and seem to be craning.

Reflexes. Some of baby's movements are out of her control and governed by reflexes; Mother Nature is pulling her "strings." If you want to bring your baby's mouth into a sucking mode, stroke the side of the face near the mouth and baby will begin to purse her mouth as if to suck. This "rooting" reflex is helpful in getting baby to the nipple. The whole upper body may jerk (the "Moro reflex" or the "startle reflex"), the arms and fingers may flail outward and then return toward the body and relax. (The baby is not nervous, but it often looks that way.) If your baby turns her head to the left, her left arm will extend and her right arm flexes up to her head. (This posture, officially known as *tonic neck reflex* is also called *the fencer's stance* because that's just what it looks like!)

A Partial List of the Newborn's Reflexes

Name	To Elicit	Baby's Movements	Possible Use to Baby
Moro, or startle	Suddenly change position, dropping baby's head backward, or make a loud noise next to baby	Throws out arms and legs, then pulls them back convulsively	Attempt to grab mother for protection, comfort
Root	Touch cheek or area around mouth	Turns head toward stimulus	Nursing aid
Suck	Touch mucous membranes inside mouth	Sucks on object	Nursing aid
Grasp	Touch palm of hand or sole of foot	Closes hand or curls foot	To hold mother while feeding, being carried

A Partial List of the Newborn's Reflexes (continued)

Name	To Elicit	Baby's Movements	Possible Use to Baby
Babinski	Stroke outside of sole of foot	Large toe curls up	Unknown
Hand to mouth	Stroke cheek *or* palm	Turns head toward stroke, bends arms up, and brings hand to mouth; mouth opens and sucks	Feeding aid; may help to clear baby's air passage
—	Shine bright light in eyes	Closes eyes	Protects eyes
Blink	Clap hands	Eyes close	Protects eyes
—	Cover mouth	Turns head away and flails arms	Prevents smothering
—	Stroke leg	Other leg crosses and pushes object away	Protection
Withdrawal	Give baby a painful stimulus	Baby withdraws	Protects body
—	Place baby on belly	Holds head up, then turns	Prevents smothering
TNR (tonic neck reflex)	Turn baby's head to side	Whole body arches away, arm and leg move to "fencing" position	Helps in birth
Step	Stand baby	Baby walks	Practice walking movements

These are all normal neurological reflexes. Your baby's movements will gradually become more deliberate; she'll be able to coordinate the use of parts of her body that now move fitfully or in response to these reflexes.

Breathing. Your baby breathes irregularly. It could be quickly for a period of 15 seconds, followed by a slow, shallow period for 5 to 10 seconds. The normal breathing pattern for a baby in the first 24 hours is about 3 or 4 times the rate of adults. (Even her heart rate is naturally almost twice yours and will slow down in about two months.) A newborn will periodically cough and sneeze in order to keep her airway clear.

Baby Care

The baby will be examined by a pediatrician within 24 hours of birth. (You may have chosen your pediatrician before the baby's birth, but if not, your obstetrician will assign one to your baby for the hospital stay.) He or she will then visit you daily and answer any questions or concerns you may have. Perhaps your doctor will share his or her own philosophy about baby care with you.

Circumcision

If you have a boy, you have to decide whether to have him circumcised. Circumcision is done in the hospital, usually on the second or third day. You must give your permission in writing in order to have it done. In some religions, it is done at home on the eighth day by a person trained in the religious rituals of circumcision.

Some benefits. Circumcision is a controversial issue, but it is currently more "fashionable" to circumcise boys. (In urban centers, at least 70% of all infant boys are circumcised.) There are some health benefits associated with being circumcised: Research shows that circumcision reduces the incidence of urinary tract infections and may even reduce the incidence of cancer of the penis and cervical cancer in his future partners.

Some risks. On the other hand, there are risks associated with any operative procedure. There is always a small risk of bleeding or infection. You are making a lifelong decision for your baby. There is also the issue of pain. (The logical assumption is that babies feel pain much as adults do. Anybody who ever accidentally hurt a baby knows that by the baby's instant cry.) It is

(more)

Circumcision, *continued*

difficult to give anesthesia around the penis without creating risks just from doing so, so more often than not no pain medication is given and alternate means of pain relief are currently being sought.

How it is done. The procedure is most often performed by the obstetrician, who is a surgeon, and not by a pediatrician. The foreskin, which is the long tube of skin that covers the head of the penis, is first carefully stretched by the obstetrician and separated from the head of the penis by gentle probing, and then removed with a scalpel. A clamp is left on the cut end for a few minutes so that there is no need for stitches. When the clamp is removed, the bleeding has already stopped.

Aftercare. After circumcision, your baby may go home with you only after he has urinated. In general, the circumcised penis requires very little aftercare. Usually a strip of gauze saturated with Vaseline® jelly is wrapped around the head of the penis so that it doesn't stick to the wound as it heals. Usually the gauze falls off after 24 hours; if not, you will be advised to remove it carefully. After that, apply more Vaseline to either a gauze pad or directly onto the inside of the diaper where it will come in contact with the penis while it completely heals over the next 2 to 4 days. This will protect the penis from rubbing against a dry surface.

While the circumcision is healing, the tissue around where the cut was made may become yellow-green in color, and might easily be mistaken for infected skin. The color is normal and to be expected. The head of a circumcised penis often has a purple-blue color, which is normal. Uncircumcised penises are also bluish at the tip, but you don't see it because the foreskin covers it.

For more information about circumcision, try visiting these helpful Web sites:

http://www.aap.org/family/circ.htm
http://www.drpaula.com/medcab/vaseline.html
http://www.drpaula.com/topics/circumcision.html
http://www.mayohealth.org/mayo/9706/htm/circumci.htm

The nurses, too, will be routinely checking on and taking care of your baby—doing some of the routine care (diapering, bathing, feeding) that you will take over very soon. Generally the baby resides in the nursery and visits you every four hours.

Baby's Firsts

Your newborn will be experiencing many "firsts" in her young life.

First Meal

For at least four hours after her birth, the baby will be on the warmer being observed and will not be fed anything. For their first feed and sometimes the second feed as well, all babies are routinely given water, just to check that the passage from mouth to stomach is clear. Generally it's plain sterile water followed by glucose water (see box below).

First Bath

At the end of the first day, your baby will get her first bath. This is often not done in front of you, unless the baby is rooming-in with you (see chapter 2). Usually a nurse gives baby the bath. A basin is filled with warm, soapy water and the baby is placed in the tub.

What is Glucose Water?

At birth, there is sometimes a dramatic decrease in baby's glucose level. You may not like the idea of your baby getting sugar water (it sounds as if your child is being given Koolaid® to drink), but glucose is part of what naturally runs through our veins.

As a matter of fact, in some cultures, shortly after birth, the midwife will prepare a solution using whatever sugar source is on hand—maybe beet sugar—and mix it with boiled water. Then she uses some kind of sponge to squeeze it directly into the baby's mouth.

This is done to prevent hypoglycemic tremors.

The nurse will vigorously wash the baby from top to bottom with a washcloth. During this first bath, the nurse will wipe off what is left of the vernix—that is, the white, sticky substance that protects the baby in utero. After the baby is cleaned, she is taken to a second basin containing fresh water or over to a big sink in the nursery to be rinsed. She will get a bath every day that she is in the nursery.

> ### What Is Vernix?
>
> Vernix seems to be a natural moisturizer and protects the skin from the fluid the baby has been floating in. It may also have antibacterial properties, which is why the vernix is not completely wiped off in the delivery room.

Baby's Eyes

The nurse will pay special attention to your baby's eyes. You will recall that ointment was put in her eyes at birth to prevent infection, but this ointment can cause the lids to become puffy and she may even develop an eye discharge. The nurses will wipe this material off the eyes and use warm water to keep the eyes clean and clear.

Baby's Umbilical Cord

Before she goes home, the plastic clamp that was put on the cord in the delivery room will be removed. The one-inch dry, twisted stump that remains will fall off in a couple of weeks.

More Tests!

During the baby's stay, she will be subjected to a variety of tests. Most hospitals, for example, do a series of very routine blood tests. In addition, some states require free screening tests that look for metabolic disorders that are detectable and treatable in newborns. A nurse or technician does these tests by drawing blood from the baby's heel—this is why you may see a Band-Aid® there on your baby. You can remove the Band-Aid after an hour or so.

Slow down the clock and cherish your baby's early moments.

One routine test measures the baby's bilirubin level, which, if elevated, is a sign of jaundice. Bilirubin is a yellow substance the body produces when breaking down red blood cells. (See the box below for more information about jaundice.)

Your baby is in a rapid phase of change these first hours and days. I strongly advise you to cherish these early moments, and whenever possible abandon preconceived notions about babies. Slow down the clock, and watch as a miraculous little person unfolds before you. Watch while your newborn moves in her own gentle dance. Both of you have a lifetime to learn all of her steps. Snap her picture daily, and label them; you will be absolutely amazed at her transformation in the days and weeks to come.

Jaundice

About one third of all newborns develop a yellow tinge to their skin by the third day of life. Sometimes doctors can predict which babies are more likely to develop jaundice by knowing your blood type and the baby's blood type. (A *Coombs test*, which determines whether your blood and your baby's blood antibodies are compatible, is done in the delivery room. If the results are positive, your bloods are incompatible and jaundice is likely.)

When you and your baby's blood pass each other in utero, some of your antibodies pass to the baby; if your blood types are not compatible, a reaction may occur that causes the red blood cells to break and release a substance called *bilirubin*. If the baby's liver is overwhelmed with a lot of this substance, jaundice occurs because bilirubin is yellow and it accumulates in the skin.

Don't be alarmed if you are told your baby is a little jaundiced. It's not a disease. The nurses will draw small samples of blood from your baby's heel 2 to 3 times a day. Usually no treatment is necessary unless the bilirubin is over 20 milligrams per deciliter of blood (20mg/dl).

(more)

Jaundice, *continued*

Treatment. Although jaundice is not remedied by giving excess amounts of water, the doctor may ask you to nurse and feed the baby more, often hoping bowel movements will follow so that some of the bilirubin can be excreted that way.

The treatment for jaundice is based on the fact that a certain wavelength of light found naturally in sunlight can help to eliminate bilirubin from the skin by breaking it down so it can be excreted in the urine and feces. Unfortunately, real sunlight also has ultraviolet radiation and can burn the baby. To treat jaundice, we use "sunlight" created by special artificial lights that break down the bilirubin so that the baby's liver doesn't have to do all the work.

"Sunning" baby is one treatment. For these treatments, the baby is undressed except for a minidiaper so that almost the entire body is available for exposure to the light. She is placed in an incubator that has clear plastic sides so the special light can shine through.

Her eyes are covered so that the light won't annoy her. Babies stay in their little "suntan parlor" except for feedings so they can spend the maximum time under these lights.

The nurses will come in and turn the baby from front to back and then later from back to front. This is baby's home until the bilirubin is at an acceptable level, usually under 12.

For reasons that are not clear, babies seem to be very calm under the lights and rarely cry. It could be because of the warmth. When you look in, it does appear that your baby is happily sunbathing.

Babies with jaundice are often kept in the hospital an extra day or two because most cases don't begin until the third day. It takes that long for the bilirubin to collect in the skin. It's also possible that jaundice may not be discovered until after discharge: Your pediatrician will handle this easily. If your baby appears yellow anytime before her two-week checkup, call the doctor.

2

The "Newborn" Mother—
The Hospital Stay

Shortly after entering the delivery room, you went from being a pregnant woman to being a mother. Congratulations again!

You remain in the delivery room for about another 15 or 20 minutes, until you have also delivered the "afterbirth" (actually the placenta). Then the doctor either stitches you up if you've had an episiotomy (an incision made by the doctor next to the vagina to allow room for the baby to emerge) or closes the incisions if you've had a Cesarean section.

The Recovery Room

Soon you will be helped onto a bed and wheeled to the recovery room. In some hospitals the baby, all cleaned up and wrapped in a blanket, will be placed in your arms and wheeled along with you. Your partner is probably right beside you as well.

After delivery, most women are taken to a recovery room, which is set aside solely for this purpose. Usually there are curtains around each bed that can be pulled around you for privacy.

Pain Returns

If you've had anesthesia, it's beginning to wear off, so you are probably experiencing some pain. Often during the pushing phase of delivery the vaginal area becomes numb so that pain is minimal. This appears to be nature's way of insuring that you continue to push hard until the baby emerges. You will start to feel pain around the vaginal opening and from any stitches that you may have needed.

Nurses will check on you periodically. When the nurse comes in, ask for ice packs, which will help stop both the pain and the bleeding; she may offer you pain relief medication such as Tylenol® as well. (If you have had your baby with you, she will soon be taken to the nursery.)

A nurse will come in and press on your abdomen to check that your uterus is contracting and to change the pads you are lying on, which may get blood-soaked. She will also take your vital signs (temperature, blood pressure, and so on). If you feel you have to urinate, ask the nurse to bring you a bedpan or to help you walk to the bathroom. Don't worry about having a bowel movement. You usually won't have one for a couple of days, until your bowel recuperates from labor.

Time for a sandwich and maybe a little champagne!

Hunger Returns

During this time you may feel hungry—it probably has been a very long time since you've eaten. Make sure your partner brings you a sandwich, if you didn't pack one. I've seen many brand-new moms eagerly washing down tuna sandwiches with a paper cup full of bubbly champagne.

Feeling Alone

Although your partner can stay with you in the recovery room, fathers often scurry out to telephone relatives and friends with the news. (Alas, there are often no phones at your recovery room bedside, and cell phones are banned because they interfere with hospital systems.) He may even run up to the nursery to find out what the baby weighs and to peek through the glass in hopes of seeing the baby again.

Many new mothers suddenly feel quite alone. Your family is not allowed into the recovery room, although they may be sitting in the waiting room. It's not uncommon for women to confide in me they feel a little "peculiar." You are experiencing some pain and you have no idea how bad it may get. You just had a baby, but you don't have her with you. You just became a mother, but where is the father? You hope that your husband will rejoin you shortly and share some news about the baby.

You will be very eager to reunite with your baby. It's important that you understand that how long you remain in the recovery room usually has very little to do with you, and everything to do with when you delivered and if your room is ready. Hospitals are, in fact, run a little bit like hotels, with checkout time about 12 noon. It takes housekeeping another hour or more to make up the room. In a busy hospital, if you delivered anytime after midnight, you may not get to your room until 2:00 P.M. the next day!

You will be both relieved and excited when you are wheeled, still in your bed, to the maternity/nursery floor. If flowers or balloons have already arrived for you, they may be next to you or tied to the rail of your bed. You will stop at the front desk of the maternity floor to check in and then you will be wheeled to your room.

Your Room

If you took a tour of the maternity floor while you were pregnant, you will have a better sense of what to expect in the way of accommodations. Most rooms have very few furnishings: a bed with handrails; a bedside table with a telephone; a rolling cart where food is put; a television set; a lamp; and a single chair, which is magically supposed to accommodate all of your visitors. Private and semiprivate rooms often have a bathroom with a shower, although sometimes the shower is down the hall.

Unless you have made arrangements for a private room, you will share your room with another woman who may not be another new mother. Your roommate may, in fact, be a pregnant woman who has been put on bedrest for a variety of reasons.

Shortly after your arrival, a nurse will come into the room and take your vital signs again. She will show you how to most comfortably get up and down from bed.

Rooming-In

In most hospitals, you will be offered the option of rooming-in. Rooming-in is the option of having your baby remain in the room with you all the time. When you are making your decision, keep in mind how brief your stay is likely to be. Hospital stays used to be seven days. Now they are commonly two days for a vaginal delivery, but could be as little as 36 hours! (If you deliver the baby 11:30 on Monday night, you will probably be discharged and gone by 12 noon on Wednesday.) If you've had a Cesarean section, you may be discharged as early as the fourth day.

If you do choose rooming-in, an isolette (a clear plastic box with baby bedding inside) is brought to your room along with a plastic bassinet. When you have visitors, instead of baby going

---

Doughnut, Anyone?

In some hospitals, a nurse will give you a "doughnut" or a cushion to sit on that provides some relief from the swelling in your vaginal area. When you want to sit up,

1. lift your knees

2. tuck the doughnut underneath your behind

3. put another pillow under your thighs

4. lean back on your elbows and then put your legs over the side of the bed

5. sit up

This *sounds* hard to do and sometimes it is, but it quickly gets easier.

More about Rooming-In

If you room-in, you either need a private room or the half of the semiprivate room that is by the window so that you will not be bothered by other people's visitors. Most hospitals try to put two rooming-in mothers in the same room whenever possible.

There will be times when the choice about rooming-in is not yours but is governed by hospital policy. For example, you won't be offered rooming-in if you've had a C-section. Even if you think you are physically up to it, the hospital can't rely on you, after this major operation, to carry the baby safely in and out of the bassinet.

Remember that you don't have to be a rooming-in mother to be a "real" mother. Even if you have not chosen rooming-in, you *can* choose to have the baby with you practically all the time. (The exception is during visiting hours when the baby will have to be returned to the nursery.) I playfully tell mothers: Ask and you shall receive—your baby. This is *your* baby: Possession and ownership resides with *you.*

back to the nursery, she goes into the isolette and remains in your room for all to see. That's strictly a matter of hospital policy. It helps prevent the spread of germs from your visitors to your newborn.

The advantage to rooming-in is that you really begin to be your baby's caretaker immediately: Everything this baby does, you see. The major disadvantage is that you are probably exhausted and could use some rest. If you can, wait to make the decision of whether or not to room-in until after the experience of delivery.

The Reunion

After a few hours, the nurses will roll the clear plastic crib on wheels, with your baby in it, into your room. They will ask you to read your identification number from your wristband. After identification, the nurse usually leaves.

What Am I Feeling?

This is the first time you two are absolutely alone—unless your partner is still with you. There are as many possible reactions at this first mother-and-baby reunion as there are mothers and

There will be a flood of emotions, from love to fear.

babies. Some women feel frightened or even disconnected. You may not immediately fall in love with the bundle in your arms. Or you may be unprepared for the rush of love you instantly feel.

The predictable pattern is for you to feel instinctively protective of your newborn and, in fact, for the newborn to calm only to *your* particular touch. There will be a flood of emotions. Typically you are bombarded with warm, loving feelings, but you may also be a little put off or even afraid of the newborn.

Some of the most anxiety-ridden mothers I've encountered were those who felt that these negative feelings were abnormal. In fact, it's all quite natural. When the fictional "Murphy Brown" was alone for the first time with her new son, she crooned her favorite, and appropriate, Aretha Franklin song, "You Make Me Feel Like a Natural Woman."

What Is My Baby Feeling?

Your baby may be in a deep, deep sleep, or she may be awake and kicking, though this is less likely. During these early moments, the baby may start to cry, and I've heard mothers ask, "What's wrong?" or "What did I do wrong?" The answer is, probably nothing.

As you will discover, babies cry for many reasons. In the crib you will find a bottle of formula or water. Or you may try breastfeeding. However, be aware that neither breast milk nor colostrum (the protein-rich first milk) appears in any quantity until the second or third day in most first-time mothers. Most babies, however, will happily suck or nuzzle against you anyway.

This is a first for both of you. Babies don't come with little instruction labels and they haven't read all the books. Be patient for both of you. Soon enough you will be actively engaged with your baby. You will become sensitive to the unique melody of your infant. After birth, although you and your baby are physically separated, you are psychically connected. There is still a strong but now invisible cord tying you to each

There is a strong but now invisible cord tying you to each other.

other. The prenatal relationship is ongoing and now growing and changing. Your newborn may soon be breastfeeding, taking nourishment directly from your body. If you are bottle-feeding, your baby still remains dependent upon you even after the actual cord is severed.

Unless you are rooming-in, your baby will be brought to you every four hours or so for feeding. If your baby was either small (less than five pounds) or large (more than nine pounds) at birth, you may be given the baby more frequently to be fed.

Feeding Your Newborn

If you are not rooming-in, you can't really know when your baby is hungry. The nurses literally have their hands full and will not bring the baby to you when she cries unless it happens to be time for feeding. The usual schedule is for the babies to feed at 10, 2, and 6, around the clock.

If you delivered early in the morning, you probably won't get to see your baby until 10 in the morning, unless you make a big fuss. (This is because of the many hospital routines that take precedence in the early part of each day.) Often it's the new father who "carries on" and is sent to the nursery to retrieve the baby.

If you are rooming-in, you can feed the baby according to the baby's needs. It is probably preferable to room-in if you want to establish breastfeeding, because the "let-down reflex" (when the glands begin getting ready to produce milk) begins in response to your baby's cry. (If you don't room-in, you can definitely still breastfeed. There will just be a little delay in getting started.) Remember, you don't make breast milk for several days after delivery.

> ### *Nighttime*
>
> Be aware that there is a big difference between daytime and nighttime at a hospital. In most hospitals your phone is turned off after nine o'clock in the evening, the lights are lower, and the staff is fewer.
>
> Some women report a tremendous surge of energy, sometimes accompanied by fear and panic, in the middle of the night. Some psychologists say the new mother is feeling depressed. It is almost as if she is grieving for the baby that was part of her body for nine months. It's also possible that the panic is simply a result, if you are not rooming-in, of not knowing what is happening to your baby.
>
> If you find yourself pacing the floor, just pace right over to the nursery. If at any time, day or night, you miss your baby, take a walk and look at what my son likes to call the "glass house for babies." You may want to take the baby back to your room, just to hold her or sing to her.

If you are not rooming-in, the nurse will automatically bring the baby to you at 2:00 A.M. unless you specifically say you don't want the baby at that time. If you are feeling up, and there is often a "high" after birth, then take the baby. There are no distractions at 2:00 A.M., no calls or visitors. But if you want to skip this visit (maybe you are feeling like you have been "to hell and back"), be sure to tell the nurse what you *do* want your baby to have. It could be water or formula. (It won't be breast milk: It is virtually impossible for you to express enough or even any breast milk during this brief time in the hospital.)

The Stay: Mother Care

As informed and ready for pregnancy and childbirth as a woman can be, no one can fully prepare you for this wonderful and yet frightening experience. Yes, it's a blessed event, but it is also often a painful and distressing experience. You are totally enveloped in what I call the "guts and glory" of new motherhood.

Labor exacts both a psychological and a physical price. For some the cost of delivering a baby is greater than for others.

Let me comfort you with the knowledge that much of what you are feeling, especially in the first 24 to 48 hours, is a result of the cacophony of hormones released when the baby is born. It's *not* all in your head. It's in your bloodstream.

After childbirth, a variety of reproductive hormones are indeed raging, coming at you from all directions. Estrogen, progesterone, oxytocin and pitocin are just some of the hormones whose balance has to be reestablished from pregnancy to postpregnancy. (It's also been observed that the level of a neural hormone called *serotonin*, which is related directly to mood, drops off just after delivery, sometimes as much as it does in people who've experienced a recent loss.)

Visitors

Keep in mind, whether you are rooming-in or not, the hospital usually limits visitors—both in number and in how long they can stay. You may think it's unfair that all the new grandparents can't come in together and coo over the baby. In fact, you may be grateful for the restrictions.

In general, most hospitals have two brief visiting periods a day. If you have other children, encourage them to visit just as soon as they can. I also advise women to bring along a picture of their older children and tape it to the inside of the newborn's crib. This is one way your new baby may be introduced to her family.

Most important, when the older siblings come to visit they will feel automatically connected to the newest member of their family. The exception to the "no visitor" rule is dad, who is usually allowed practically to room-in himself.

Labor often leaves you with a lot of mostly temporary physical ills. You may be hypertensive, hypoglycemic and bloated. Some new mothers mistakenly believe that childbirth will immediately "cure" some of the ailments they suffered during pregnancy. But, for example, it takes at least 48 hours after birth for nasal discomfort and congestion to disappear. (I've heard more than one mom ask, "How come my nose is still stuffed?") And it can take weeks for a pregnancy rash to fade.

Going to the Bathroom

The first time you try to have a bowel movement may be quite painful. You are not sure you won't just break open and fall apart. You won't, but you may leak some blood. And when you urinate it might not be in a single stream the way it used to be—it may be more like a shower. This will change. (The nurses will encourage you to drink lots of liquid so that you urinate frequently.) You'll usually feel more comfortable if you hold your hand or a pillow firmly against your abdomen while you are urinating or having a bowel movement. You may be offered a laxative, which can make the difference between a hard and difficult stool or a soft and easier one. If it's still painful, tell your doctor.

Hemorrhoids

Many women leave the delivery room with a brand new baby and a brand new case of hemorrhoids. Even if you had a C-section, unless it was totally planned, there was still a lot of pushing, from which you may indeed get hemorrhoids. About one third of women wind up with hemorrhoids after delivery. Some cases are more bothersome than others. The nurses will usually give you an inflatable seat or "doughnut" to sit on when you go to the bathroom so you don't hurt as much when you push. Stool softeners are also helpful. In some cases your doctor may prescribe a cream to help shrink your hemorrhoids.

Walk!

It's important to start walking as soon as you can after delivery. When you do stand up, you will probably notice that you still look pregnant. After I delivered my first child, I became impatient in the recovery room, so I abused my "doctor's privileges" and walked up the staff staircase to the nursery. I literally bumped into a fellow doctor who asked, "When are you due?" That dealt a momentary blow to my vanity!

Weighing In

I recommend that you walk to the nursery as much as you like, but *not* over to the scale. The baby, the placenta and the amniotic fluid added all together only weigh about 12 pounds. You probably have at least another 20 to "explain away." There will also be a lot of fluid shifting, so I suggest you wait at least a week before weighing in. To make yourself feel better during your stay: Wash your hair, put on makeup or whatever it takes so you feel as lovely as everyone says the new baby is.

Cesarean Sections

Cesarean sections (C-sections) present a different set of challenges to a new mom. In an elective or planned C-section, a small horizontal incision, around 4 inches in length, is made at the lower part of the abdomen. If you had what we call a *crash* or *emergency C-section*, then the scar runs up and down and may appear quite long. In either case, the trend is to help you sit up and walk the same or the very next day.

Recovery time. C-section mothers often feel pretty good the very next day and then lousy two days later. If you hadn't been pushing and going through the several stages of labor for hours and hours, then you may

> In the past, C-section women stayed in the hospital up to two weeks and didn't get up out of bed until the fourth day. Today you can expect to get out of the hospital on the fourth day.

The typical C-section scar is small and follows the "bikini line." The longer vertical scar in emergency Cesarean procedures will also heal well in time.

even feel "up" for the first day or so after the delivery. Usually you are able to walk to the bathroom—though you may be afraid your stitches will "burst open"—and it's easier to have a bowel movement if you've had a C-section.

The discomfort on the second day has to do with the natural healing process. When the stitches are fresh and holding together nicely, you tend to feel better than when the scar is actually forming and the stitches start tugging and contracting. (The skin heals by knitting together, and that process hurts.) By the second day, you may need pain relief. There are a variety of pain medications that you can take, and you should request one when you are hurting.

Take special care of your health now. The biggest difference between a C-section and a vaginal delivery is that you have had a major operation and you need to take special care of your own health. You may opt for a nurse to help you at home. Going back to your regular life—exercising, driving a car, even bathing—is postponed longer.

Dealing with Emotions

In addition to the physical scars, a C-section sometimes leaves behind very painful psychological ones. Childbirth classes rarely discuss C-sections and usually dismiss them with a sentence or two as if they rarely happen. Understand that C-sections account for at least one third of all deliveries in the United States. I've heard new mothers say, "I went through all that labor for *nothing*," losing sight that they didn't go through it for nothing but for that precious bundle that is now in their arms.

C-sections account for at least one third of all deliveries in the United States.

Often women have the feeling that they have somehow failed if they had a C-section. In my new-mother groups, I hear that sentiment echoed over and over. One mom said, "My friend was pregnant at the same time I was, and she said, 'Well, I wouldn't *let* a C-section happen to me.'" (Obviously, a C-section is not something you "let happen to you" but is medically necessary.) However, mothers who've had a real struggle getting pregnant or going full term don't much care *how* they had the baby.

Breast Milk after C-Section

You probably will not have breast milk or colostrum until the third, fourth or even fifth day. Why does it take longer for your milk to come in than it does after a vaginal delivery?

When you are in pain, which is a form of stress, the body's response is to decrease the release of the hormone that is responsible for initiating the flow of milk. Even so, if you are not yet making milk and you are planning to breastfeed, you should be "practicing." It's a good learning experience for the baby to suck and for you to find comfortable positions.

You can also enlist the father's help in positioning the baby for breastfeeding by placing pillows under your arms or by demonstrating the "football position." In the football position, baby lies along your side with legs out back and head lowered to the breast.

Going Home

On your last day in the hospital, your nurse will give you a
document with vital information for you to keep and another
paper for you to fill out. The first will list the baby's birth weight,
length and blood type. The second asks you to name the baby.
Don't feel pressured into choosing a name. All you need to do is
write *Baby Girl Cohen* or *Baby Boy O'Brien*. It's not essential to
name the baby at that moment. Later you can request a form from
your state's registry to give your baby a proper name.

The night before you are expecting to be discharged, send
home with your partner any flowers, balloons or gifts you have
received. Make sure you have clothes to go home in: Do *not* have
your partner bring you your regular-size jeans! You will do better
to go home in something comfortable, such as a sweatpants outfit
that would fit a 6-months-pregnant woman.

At some point during your stay, there should be the
opportunity to watch bathing and feeding demonstrations
conducted by nurses. If you are not invited, make sure to ask to
be included.

Leaving a Jaundiced Baby Behind

A word about leaving: If you know your baby is jaundiced,
you may have to leave the hospital without her. It's a very
disappointed and sad mother who goes home without her
beautiful birthday package.

Remember that jaundice is *not* a disease and, for the
short time you are separated, you can visit her as often as
you like. If, however, you are not feeling completely well,
you can talk to your obstetrician about staying an extra
day. More often than not, the baby only has to stay one
extra day—if it's more than that, you will be discharged
before the baby is.

Layette for the First 6 to 8 Weeks

Clothing

3 dozen cloth or disposable diapers (or 1 dozen cloth if using
  disposables, to use as spit-up wipers)
3-6 pair cloth diaper cover-ups (Velcro®-type closures preferable)
6-12 newborn undershirts
6-8 short-sleeved tops or long "kimonos" for warm weather
6-8 newborn jumpsuits for cool weather and nights
2-4 warm buntings or sleep suits for daytime outings and nighttime
  sleeping in cold weather
1-2 sun hats (warm weather)
1-2 warm hats (cold weather)
2-3 washable booties or socks
1-2 very small sweaters, preferably cotton

Bedding

6-12 receiving blankets
3-4 sets of rubber pads and soaker mats to change baby on and
  protect laps and sheets
3-6 crib sheets
2-3 baby towels, extra soft, absorbent, possibly with a hood
3-6 baby washcloths
2-4 medium-weight, washable blankets

Supplies

Mild soap with moisturizer for bathing the baby
Mild soap for washing the baby's clothes
Diaper bucket
Rectal thermometer
Petroleum jelly and diaper-rash ointment, with zinc oxide
2-3 pacifiers
Small, somewhat stiff hairbrush
Formula (for bottle-fed babies): small cans or powder for travel
6-8 bottles and nipples for water, formula or expressed breast milk

Equipment

Bassinet
Bottle brush
Cradle, carriage or crib for the baby to sleep in
Dresser or shelves to store the baby's clothes
Padded, secure changing table or surface
Small square plastic basin or baby bathtub
Infant chest carrier
Infant car safety seat
Portable bed or carry basket
Tote bag for diapers, extra clothes, etc.

When it's time to leave, you will need a receiving blanket and an outfit that has been washed in advance for the baby. Some infant clothes are stiff with sizing and need to be prewashed. (Use a detergent that will not destroy the flame-retardant properties in baby's clothes. It should say "flame-retardant-safe" right on the box.)

Find out what the hospital discharge time is. Make sure you give yourself at least an hour to dress the baby. The inner clothes, including the undershirt, should be 100% cotton. Make sure the outfit you choose has legs rather than a "sac" style, so that you can easily get her into an infant car seat (the law in every state). Many people find this out the hard way, on their knees in the back seat trying desperately to stuff a baby in a blanket sleeper into a car seat. In some climates, you need a cotton hat for baby.

If you are adopting a baby, you might find this Web site helpful:

http://www.adopting.org/ar.html

The morning you are going to leave, the pediatrician will come in and deliver a speech on baby care, covering anything and everything—from feeding to bathing and diapering. Or she might hand you some pamphlets. Have a pad and paper ready to write down any questions that come up. Before you leave, it's important to ask what the baby's weight at discharge is. It will give you perspective when you see the pediatrician two weeks later.

All kinds of paperwork is exchanged among the doctors and the nurses. Then the moment will come when the nurse will ask: "Are you ready?" You may think, "Not really." The nurses will check your armband and your baby's band one last time and hand you a copy of the birth certificate. It also lists the baby's birth weight and the certificate number that you have been

You Aren't Going Anywhere without a Car Seat for Baby

You will have to have an approved car seat to take your baby home in before the hospital will release your baby. It's the law.

For more information about choosing and installing approved car seats, visit these Web sites:

http://www.drpaula.com/topics/carseat.html

http://www.aap.org/family/carseat3.html

reading off to the nurse each time they brought you the baby. You will be handed a small folder, which you will use later to record your baby's immunizations and doctor visits. The hospital may give you some formula, if you've been using it, and sometimes a gift basket filled with baby-care products.

You may even have to deal with the cashier's office before you can take home your baby. In some hospitals, you must sit in a wheelchair with the baby on your lap until you exit the hospital door. More commonly, you are escorted out on foot with your baby in your arms. It's an incredible, private moment when you take possession of your baby. You come out of the hospital with a big, special present—your baby.

You are on your way home.

It's time to say goodbye to the hospital and hello to your new life.

Part II

Tender Loving Care—
Mothers

3

Homecoming—
The New Family

If time seemed to slow down in the delivery room, when you arrive home it may seem upside down and inside out. New mothers may feel like Alice in the looking glass. They experience wonder and puzzlement as they see a reflection in the mirror of someone they are not yet familiar with. I tell mothers, "You leave the house an expectant mother and you come home a mommy!"

Reality Sets In

The door shuts. You are home. Looking back at this moment, most women recall having a lot to do. I clearly remember walking into my apartment with the baby in my arms and thinking, "I have to check the answering machine for messages. Do the plants need watering? Is there enough milk in the refrigerator? Has the dog been walked today?" I was concerned with all the details of our daily life. I found myself behaving the way I always did when I walked in the door. In addition to everything else I worry about, having a new baby added one more thing to my "to do" list. The world on my shoulders had just gotten heavier!

At my new-mother groups, many moms confess that the first hours home from the hospital were not as "magical" as they had imagined. The fantasy of the fairy tale-like entrance was replaced with visions of responsibilities dancing in their heads. As one mom said, "I walked in the door and I heard myself shouting, 'Why are all the dishes still in the sink?' and 'Where's the bassinet?'"

Special Moments

Friends and relatives may want to be there for your homecoming. However, this is a special, private moment that occurs only once with this baby. Many moms tell me that the last thing they wanted when they got home was a parade of people coming to admire the baby. But that's just what they got.

My suggestion is that when you first come home, forget the chores and go into the room where your baby will be sleeping, possibly your own bedroom. Unplug the phone. Close the door. I strongly recommend that you spend the next few hours in that environment. This little interlude is a gift for you, your baby and your mate. Being alone with each other now is often more important in terms of bonding than was the actual moment of birth.

New mothers who take these hours for themselves are overwhelmingly glad they did. But don't be surprised if you are accused of being selfish, silly or neurotic by all of those friends and relatives to whom you said, "I want to be alone!" If necessary, say it was your pediatrician's advice.

After a few hours, when your baby has gradually become accustomed to the sight and sounds of her room, you can introduce her to the rest of her home. Take your baby for a tour

Be Honest with Yourself and Others

In the hospital, think about what kind of homecoming you want. If you decide you want to be alone, then specifically ask friends and relatives not to be there.

When I discussed this with an expectant couple recently, the mom-to-be nudged her husband and said, "I told you your mother doesn't need to be there." Yet, there are other women who specifically want their own mothers to be there for them. A brand-new mom may be very proud to share being a mother with her own "mommy."

It's Cultural

It is, in fact, natural to isolate yourself with your baby for a while. In many cultures, the mother and baby are assigned to a midwife or assistant, who helps them with the transition from birth to afterbirth. They live separated from the community for up to six weeks. This may have started as part of some superstitious beliefs. But anthropologists, including the late Margaret Mead, have suggested that this custom may have evolved in order to insure that new mothers get what they really need: Time alone with the baby and away from responsibilities.

of the house and make the world a familiar place to her. Soon enough the television, radio, neighbors and relatives will intrude and distract you.

Introducing Baby and Pet

Don't be surprised if your faithful family pet isn't too eager to share his space with a new arrival. It's a good idea to get the pet used to the new baby even *before* you come home.

Your partner could bring home a T-shirt that the baby has worn in the hospital. That will help your pet acquire a smell for the baby. When they meet for the first time, you don't want your pet to howl or hide.

Call the Doctor

I also recommend that at the end of the first 24 hours you touch base with your pediatrician. When I say good-bye on my final visit before discharge, I tell the new mother to keep a pad by her side and jot down any questions that come up after she leaves the hospital. I suggest she call me in 24 hours. She usually says, "Oh, I'll only call if I have questions." Enough questions generally accumulate after 24 hours to warrant a chat.

No Routine Is the Routine

It's a good time, after these first 24 hours at home, to sit back and take a big breath. When I ask the mother how she is doing, I invariably hear a great big sigh! I often find that the mother, in that first day home, has been searching for patterns to rely on. But what she has discovered is that there *aren't any yet.* Instead, you need to accept unpredictability.

Your baby is very different today than she was just yesterday. I smile when the mother of a 1-week-old says, "But she used to sleep for 3 hours at a time," or "She used to have a bowel movement once a day." It's too early for any predictable patterns to have developed. Your baby may at times be very wakeful or very sleepy, very hungry or suddenly fussy. All of this is perfectly normal for newborns. You will soon enough come to know your baby and how to make a space for her in your life.

Simplify

I always give this advice: *Simplify your life.*
Here are some ideas for making it happen:

- Tell yourself in advance that you are not going to earn an "A" for every task.

- Decide you are not going to bother with the laundry. (Try to be sure there's a week's supply of clean clothes before you leave for the hospital.)

- Remember all those friends and relatives who asked if there was anything they could do for you? Tell them yes. Make a list *before* you even go to the hospital.

- Maybe a friend could straighten up the apartment before you get there. It may be a mess, and you don't want to have to coordinate details from the hospital.

- Does someone need to assemble whatever furniture may have been delivered?

- Have someone greet the baby nurse (if you are having one). You probably don't want to meet her at the hospital.

Letting in the Rest of the World

Soon enough the time will come when you throw open your doors and welcome the friends, neighbors and relatives who want to celebrate the newest member of your family. There is tremendous pleasure and pride in showing off your baby to others. It's hard for adults to pass up caressing a newborn.

It's hard for adults to pass up caressing a newborn.

Advice from Others

Well-meaning relatives will want to share with you all of their own experiences, which may or may not be helpful. My advice is to listen with one ear, smile and take it with a grain of salt. You need to experience your baby for yourself.

Child-rearing notions change and people have distorted memories. People often remember parenting the way they wish it had been and not necessarily the way it actually was. My mother-in-law often recalled that her son slept through the night when he was only one week old and spoke at six months! I recently overheard a mother of a teenager saying, "Oh, when my son was a baby, he never cried. He just looked at me and I knew exactly what he wanted."

My advice is to trust your own instincts. This is *your* baby. So don't be intimidated by your mother, mother-in-law, best friend or your baby nurse.

> *Go to this Web site for a list of "must-have" newborn medical cabinet requirements:*
>
> **http://www.drpaula.com/medcab/babymed.html**

Not Just "Parents Only"

Recently there seems to be a return to the old belief that newborns shouldn't be picked up or touched by anyone but the parents. I don't subscribe to that. Obviously if a friend has a cold

> ### Golden Rules for Parents
>
> *My #1 Golden Rule for Parents is:* Babies are not fragile.
> I must get thousands of questions that stem from the
> underlying sense that babies are fragile and can splinter like
> glass. Although they *appear* to be soft and vulnerable
> creatures, they are really pretty tough. Even the so-called
> "soft spot" is covered by a thick membrane.
>
> *My #2 Golden Rule for Parents is:* Babies are not sterile.
> They don't need to be handled with surgical gloves. You will
> save a lot of precious time, for instance, if you don't rewash
> everything of baby's that touches the carpet.

she shouldn't pick up the baby. Toddlers in particular should have
limited access to the newborn. That's simply because toddlers are
famous for breaking out in chickenpox or strep throat or the very
common cold just hours after they've visited you. And their
hygiene leaves a lot to be desired. But no matter what, if it's
your toddler who wants to pick up her new baby brother, then
go for it (with supervision, of course). It's part of the package of
being a family.

New Roles

You not only became a mother when you were handed your
newborn, you automatically became part of a new extended
family. There can be a wonderful sense of symmetry to the
continuing life cycle. When one of my new mothers broke her
arm, she called her own father to help her with the baby, because
her husband was out of town. Her father rushed right over. As
this mom put it, "It occurred to me that once you become a
parent, you are a parent forever. Even though I now have a baby
of my own, I will always be my daddy's child. That was really
nice to know."

Grandparents

You will undoubtedly have a different relationship with your own parents. Grandparents often claim "ownership" of the new baby and can step over imaginary boundaries as they stake out their territorial rights. (As one woman explained, "It's not surprising that my parents want to be around a lot. My son has my father's name.") New mothers occasionally find they now have a somewhat tense relationship with their own mothers. I hear new mothers complaining they feel

> On the positive side, try to see grandparents as the people who will love, cherish (and baby-sit) your baby.

"infantilized"—treated as if they are suddenly not competent or capable of taking care of a baby. The torrent of advice can be unwanted and even insulting. ("You must be doing something wrong. You never cried when you were a baby.")

Don't be too quick to give thumbs down to all of their advice. Maybe your mother has a different way of holding your daughter

Twins can be twice the pleasure, but expect more than twice the work at times. Be creative and don't hesitate to ask for help when you need it.

that really seems to soothe her. Try not to pounce every time your mother intervenes. Let's say your son has hiccups, which doesn't concern you in the least. But your mother jumps up, dips her finger in sugar and then puts it in your son's mouth. You may be horrified at the scene, but your mother is just repeating what *her* mother taught her. Both you and your baby can "swallow" (or at least tolerate) most of your parents' advice.

In-Laws

Don't be surprised if your in-laws suddenly elevate your status. As one mother explained, "I had a very neutral relationship with my in-laws until I gave them their little 'prince.' Then it all changed. They are much nicer as grandparents than they were as in-laws." They are also around more often. Unfortunately the extra attention—the daily phone calls and surprise visits—is not always welcome. Hopefully you'll all learn to strike an acceptable balance.

Friends

Your relationship with friends who don't have children will not be the same. You are now on different sides of the looking glass!

Initially friends will come to visit bearing balloons and gifts. One mother sadly reported that a good friend came over to meet the baby and never came back again. She also reluctantly admitted that yes, the baby was the focus of the entire evening.

> You may find yourself drawn closer to the friends who already have children. They'll love you for asking advice and will welcome you into the informal mommy club.

Most women without children are not fascinated with the details of baby care. As another friend said to a new mother, "Do you realize how boring you've become?" "Boring" probably wasn't the right word. "Consumed" with her new daughter would be more accurate.

Old friends are not quite sure how to treat you. They ask you to go out to the movies on Saturday night as usual, and you think, "I'd rather be home with my baby." If they invite you over for dinner, they may be concerned that you will bring the baby. And you may be offended if they don't include the baby. At the same time, they may not realize how hard it is for you to get a sitter—and that you might not want to get one just yet.

It's almost as if you speak different languages. A single friend Beth complained to me about her friend Nora who had become a mother. Nora went to the theater and when she called home, the sitter said the baby wouldn't stop crying. Nora immediately called Beth and asked her to go over and check that the baby was really all right. Beth went reluctantly, but she was annoyed almost beyond words at her "paranoid" and inconsiderate friend. She didn't understand at all until a few years later when she had her first child.

Reach out and make your old friends comfortable.

There's no question that you will have to reach out and make your old friends comfortable. Preserve those relationships that are worth saving. These first few months are critical as to whether a particular friendship will even continue. You may find yourself drawn closer to the friends who already have children. They'll love you for asking advice and will welcome you into the informal mommy club.

Making New Friends

Becoming a new mother is a great opportunity to make lots of new friends. Don't be afraid to look a woman with a baby directly in the eye and start a conversation. When you were pregnant, strangers often broke the social ice with, "When are you due?" Now you can simply ask, "How old is your baby?"

Long days can be made to seem much shorter when they are shared with another mother and baby. You may almost feel like you are back in kindergarten. You meet "neat" kids (of all ages). You get to play with toys. You get to go to the park and the zoo.

The New Father

In the elevator in the hospital recently, I watched as a couple went home with their newborn. The father was lovingly cradling the baby, when the mother reached for her. The dad said, "You carried her for nine months, let me have a turn." Dads are parents too, but often we neglect the new dad and all of his feelings.

In my office, one expectant father asked a new father, "How does life change after the baby?" The new father replied, "Life doesn't change. You just start a whole new one."

It would be a great loss to your baby and to the father for him to be left out. Babies benefit from the love and care of both parents. Tender-loving care can be dispensed by dads. Most dads are willing to participate, even if they look to mom for guidance. Unfortunately, dads are often relegated to the role of observer. You don't bond by having philosophical discussions. You bond by taking care of your baby—by changing his diaper and having him

The marital spotlight shifts from the couple and shines on the baby.
It's usually the mother who controls the beam.

smile when you nuzzle his stomach. If you say, "My husband doesn't like to do those sort of things, so I do it," you are cheating everyone.

A father, however, is not a male mother. Fathers father differently than mothers mother. Although there are a lot of things you can both do, the style with which you do them is different. Your baby will benefit from the differences.

> A mother who realized her son needed her husband's attention as well as her own marveled, "I can see him falling in love with my husband."

So, when dad is with the baby, don't peek over his shoulder to see if he's doing it "right." He's nervous too and may think you were somehow born with a diapering or bathing gene!

It is difficult for your husband to be left out of a relationship that is clearly pleasurable to you. Force yourself to let go and let him derive the same pleasures you get from bathing the baby, even diapering and all that kissing and snuggling.

Remember that your husband returned from the hospital in a new role, just as you did. He just didn't have the same dramatic body changes, although he may have gained a few pounds eating along with you. (I recently conducted a little survey and discovered the average weight gain for fathers was about six pounds!)

Let Him Do the Loving, Too

I've said it before and it's worth repeating: Women get angry with fathers for not participating in the "hard" part of parenting. But sometimes mothers don't let fathers in to do the "easy" and wonderful part—the loving.

Your husband can't grow to be attached to the baby unless he has a lot of physical contact. Help him be part of the new trio. You can all lie on the bed together and cuddle. It really is delicious to have all the people you love the most right beside you. Savor these precious moments.

During the evolution of this new life, the creation of the relationship with the baby is all-consuming. The marital spotlight shifts from the husband and shines on the baby. It's usually the wife who controls the beam. The husband experiences this period differently, but he has valid experiences of his own.

4

The Fourth Trimester

Some pregnant women imagine that after birth their bodies will quickly turn back 9 months, like the resetting of a clock. Of course, it's not like that at all. The truth is, you've replaced one set of discomforts for another. When you were pregnant, you went to the bathroom practically all the time. Now you don't go nearly as often, but your bladder control is poor. You spent sleepless nights trying to find a comfortable position. Now you can find the position, but you still have sleepless nights because the baby keeps getting up.

It was easier to be pregnant than to be the mother of a newborn.

I remember that after my first child was born I almost wished the baby were back inside of me. It was easier to be pregnant than to be the mother of a newborn. This is often referred to as the *postpartum period*. I prefer to call it the *fourth trimester*. (In medical terms, pregnancy is divided into three 3-month periods. They are the first, second and third trimesters, and at the end you give birth.)

How well you survive the fourth trimester has a lot to do with your *expectations* for both your physical and psychological well-being. Try not to pay too much attention to your neighbor who bounced back from pregnancy and went back to work in three days, or to your hospital bedmate who zipped up her size-6 jeans and waltzed out of bed. There really is a wide range of normal recovery patterns, and you probably will fall somewhere in the middle. It's been my experience that the vast majority of new mothers are *not* zipping up their jeans and dashing off to work. But those exceptions are the ones that grab our attention.

Tender Loving Care:
Your Psychological Needs

On the psychological front, much of what you are feeling is still under hormonal regulation. As a result of your hormone swings, you may be prone to strong emotions. For reasons that are not entirely clear, these are usually negative emotions. The feelings we typically associate with the postpartum period are

- insecurity (such as waking up in the middle of the night, and deciding that everything you have bought for the baby is somehow wrong)
- sadness (including crying jags)
- anger
- irrational fear (such as deciding that your next-door neighbor is really Jack the Ripper incarnate)

It's as if your body is in a constant state of vigilance. These feelings are hormonally programmed reactions, probably

---

Protect!

No matter what other feelings you are experiencing, you will automatically protect this new baby of yours in ways you cannot even imagine.

A new mother recently came out of the hospital with her infant in her arms and tripped on the stairs (a very uncommon occurrence). Normally a person would put her arms out to break her fall. But this woman stopped herself with her face and was rewarded with a broken nose.

Only her pediatrician totally understood that this woman, now a mother, could not, would not, thrust her arms forward and let her baby fall! (Mother and baby are now doing just fine.)

Periods of detachment or sadness are not uncommon in the first weeks after delivery, particularly at those moments when it is difficult to satisfy your baby. These short, but intense, episodes are known as "baby blues."

designed to help the mother protect her precious little one. Your hormonal changes are similar to the changes that occur in what's known as the *fright/flight phenomenon:* Your body is ready to "defend," "attack" or "flee" depending on the situation. This is the state the new mother often finds herself in. She is anxious and ready to leap.

The Baby Blues

You may mistakenly label this period as "postpartum depression." However, postpartum depression is a specific, serious illness (see box, page 63). What you most likely have is a case of the "baby blues," which is a state of mind and not an illness.

You can console yourself that much of what you do while experiencing the blues is reversible. Almost anything you say will be forgiven, if not instantly forgotten. New mothers often display the symptoms of the baby blues to anyone who is around. So one mother may say, "I wish I never had this baby." Another will accuse her own mother, "You don't know anything about raising

Sometimes the pain and letdown after delivery can overshadow the experience.

a baby!" (as if she hadn't raised you). Yet another mom will turn to her husband and complain, "You don't understand, and you're never here when I need you."

These outbursts can come on uncontrollably, a little bit as if you were possessed by a "Harpy." However, rarely do they have any lasting impact on the development of your family. Let me assure you that this brief period will pass. Most husbands are forgiving. I like to joke, "If you find yourself bewitched and bothered, your husband is probably more than a little 'bewildered' himself."

New-Mothers Groups

No matter how lousy you may feel, it's particularly important that you don't isolate yourself from others. If you can, this is the

I like this Web site for its self-help suggestions for new mothers after the pregnancy:

**http://www.alexian.org/progserv/babies/mothercare/
mothercare.html#index**

perfect time to join a new-mothers group. (Call your pediatrician, obstetrician or childbirth educator for leads, and check bulletin boards in doctors' offices as well.)

When I run groups, mothers often say, "I wish I had been here the first week after I got home."

Sharing feelings is a wonderful antidote to the blues.

What's crucial is the acknowledgment that what one mother is feeling is being shared by almost all of the mothers. Sharing feelings is a wonderful antidote to the blues. It's important to realize that you can be thrilled and delighted with your newborn *and* exhausted and resentful at the same time. One feeling doesn't negate the other. Motherhood is never an either/or proposition.

"Invisible Woman"

It was at one of my new-mothers groups that a mother first confessed that she felt like an "invisible woman." As she said that, mothers around the room nodded their heads in agreement. A strange, but not scientifically proven, phenomena often happens as soon as the baby is born: Moms slowly fade. Even in the hospital, everyone rushes over to the nursery.

As one mom said, "I remember thinking, what about me? I'm part of the birth day, too." Now that a few weeks have passed, that same mother lamented, "I'm thinking of going on vacation, since I feel superfluous. Nobody ever asks me how I am."

I recently visited a new mother and baby in the hospital, and the mother asked her husband to bring her a hair dryer so she could "do" her hair. Her husband responded, "Why? No one will be looking at you."

Be good to yourself every opportunity you get.

You will have to find your own ways to color yourself back into life. Be good to yourself every opportunity you get. This is a good time to start meditating, to give yourself a few minutes to clear your head and adjust to your new life. Or do yoga. Play music you really like.

Use any free time to spend a few quiet, peaceful moments.
Meditation and yoga are just two of many ways to relax.

Rent happy movies. And make sure you smile whenever you pass another mother. Empathy really works wonders in the healing process.

Tender Loving Care: Your Physical Needs

Don't neglect yourself. Even if you feel like you have no time for yourself, find the time. Looking good makes you feel better when those uninvited friends show up. (And they *will* show up, protesting, "I know you didn't mean *me* when you said no visitors.")

As I've said, your body does not miraculously return to its prenatal state, though you might assume it should. This misconception is fueled by society. There's even a "pregnant doll" on the market. After the baby "pops out," the stomach immediately becomes flat as a board!

Postpartum Depression

Postpartum depression (PPD) is a real illness with its own symptoms. It is a significant, though little-written-about condition. It differs from "baby blues" both in severity and in symptoms, though some overlap exists and can lead to a delay in diagnosis.

For a long time, PPD was discarded as not being a "real" condition. Women who found themselves with symptoms were considered to have underlying psychiatric instability that the stress of motherhood happened to uncover. No wonder so few women ever sought help until recently.

PPD is estimated to occur in 2 per 3,000 deliveries, which translates to about 370,000 women in the United States each year. PPD is the hormonally and biochemically induced reaction to the body's upheaval in giving birth. Its symptoms coincide with the sudden and dramatic drop in progesterone and estrogen levels and the similar reduction in neural hormones and endorphins. Even the thyroid and adrenal hormones (cortisone), which have been pumping throughout pregnancy, take a dive. All this drama begins within 24 to 36 hours of delivery.

The symptoms of PPD may include
- anxiety
- paranoia
- detached feelings (particularly from the baby)
- sleeplessness
- loss of appetite
- loss of sexual desire
- uncontrollable crying
- hallucinations
- suicidal behavior

In its severest form, it usually leads to hospitalization.

On the other hand, "baby blues" usually has some relationship to the circumstances around the birth (difficult delivery, a C-section when you were determined not to have one, too many responsibilities). It is often limited to mildly depressive symptoms and tearfulness. A woman may experience self-doubt and a lack of enthusiasm over her new role, but nothing like the passionate depths of despair associated with PPD.

Usually all the major symptoms have resolved by the fourth month, but the memories of this time may last a lifetime.

Hygiene and Aftercare

Personal cleanliness was probably something you always took for granted. Of course you want to be clean and well groomed, but now you have to renegotiate on your body's terms.

Showers, not baths. In the first weeks, showering is preferable to bathing, and you really shouldn't bathe until the doctor tells you it's all right. You may need your partner to help you get in and out of the shower. Many new mothers leak breast milk in the shower and feel more comfortable wearing a bra.

> **Advice**
>
> You never know when you will bleed, or how much bleeding there will be, so wear a sanitary napkin and avoid wearing white clothes for the first few weeks.

Vaginal care. You have to pay particular attention to your vaginal area. For general hygiene there are pads saturated with witch hazel known as "Tucks," which both cleanse and soothe. Every time you go to the bathroom, squirt warm water on your vaginal area. You may have been given a little plastic squirt bottle in the hospital. I continued to use that bottle for weeks after I got home. After I squirted the water, I would see little clots of blood in the toilet bowl, which is perfectly normal.

All new mothers, even C-section mothers, experience some vaginal bleeding. Vaginal bleeding is hormonal, the shedding of the lining of the uterus.

Bladder control. Your bladder control may be poor, and you may leak a little urine. Practice stopping your urine stream by tightening your muscles (Kegel exercises). Empty your bladder often. As your uterus shrinks it relieves the pressure on the bladder, which leads to a natural return of function.

Stitches and Other Ailments

Pay particular attention to all of your body parts that were affected by the birth.

Stitches. If you had a C-section, your stitches, which were removed in the hospital, still need some attention. The best way to clean your scar or healing wound is to use a soapy washcloth.

1. Wet the washcloth and squeeze it over your abdomen so that the soapy water runs down over the stitches. Don't rub the scar or it could hurt or disrupt the scab that is forming.

2. Use the washcloth and rinse again with clear water, or just let the shower water run over you.

3. If you had an episiotomy, treat it as you would the incision in a C-section. Squeeze the washcloth over the area and use a spray bottle.

Once you are permitted to take a bath, the general rule is: The more swelling, the more you should use cold water; the less swelling, the better warm water feels. (You may also discover that sitting on hard surfaces feels better than soft.)

Breasts. Your breasts need special attention whether or not you are breastfeeding. If you are breastfeeding, your nipples may be tender and the breasts engorged. As baby sucks, the nipple gets leathery and more accustomed to the action. The rest of the

Your breasts need special attention whether or not you are breastfeeding.

breast may be rocky hard and you may see big blue veins around the center of the chest. That's just evidence of the increased blood supply that your breasts require for production of milk.

Painful engorgement can be relieved with cool packs. Just fill some zip-type plastic bags with ice cubes. (See "When Milk Comes In," page 84, for special care of breasts.)

If you are breastfeeding, you may also feel hot. It is quite normal to run a slight temperature of 99F/37.2C to 100F/37.7C. If your temperature goes over 100.6 F/38.1C, if your breast throbs with pain, or there are warm red areas on either breast, call the doctor. It's probably a blocked milk duct, which may need more attention and possibly medication.

Even if you are not breastfeeding, you may have some discomfort. Don't be surprised if your breasts are a bit swollen even a week after birth. Although you are bottle-feeding, it takes your body a while to figure that out and to stop producing the hormones that turn on milk production. Since there is no demand for milk, there will be no supply. Your breasts will shrink back but you may still have stretch marks.

Hemorrhoids. Unfortunately, your hemorrhoids may have traveled home with you from the hospital. Until you can take a real bath, try sitting in a baby bathtub filled with water and placed on the closed toilet seat. Use the towel bar as a brace to lower yourself. (Invariably, just as you get into the tub, maybe with a book on your knees, the phone rings! Turn the ringer off before you attempt a bath.)

It's important that you keep your stools soft. If the doctor encouraged you to continue to take prenatal vitamins, your stools may be hard because the vitamins are high in iron. Take stool softeners and drink lots and lots of fluid to help keep your stools from hardening.

Remember, the harder you push, the bigger and more swollen and tender those hemorrhoids become. Apply either an over-the-counter hydrocortisone cream or hemorrhoid preparation. If necessary, your doctor will prescribe a stronger cream to help shrink them.

Taking Inventory from Head to Toe

If you stand naked in front of a full-length mirror, you can see the inevitable and predictable changes in your body. You may be reluctant to stand in front of the mirror due to these very same changes!

Hair

Start with your hair. You may experience sudden loss. Try not to use harsh products, and use a detangler or conditioner so your hair won't pull out or break as easily. Consider a new, shorter haircut.

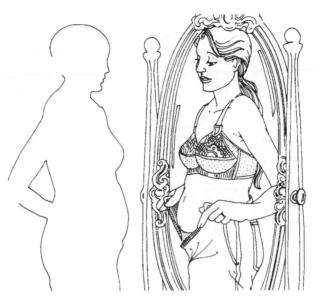

*Don't expect to slip right into your pre-pregnancy clothing.
Understand that your body needs time to return to what it was.*

Skin

You may find you have brown spots on your face. Be careful not
to expose your skin to the sun. Your skin will soon return to
normal, but it will be drier during this period, and you may need
extra moisturizer.

Some women develop skin moles or get rashes during or right
after pregnancy. Usually these disappear on their own within a
few weeks or months.

Sinuses

You may feel as if you have a cold or just a stuffed nose. This may
be due to postpartum sinus swelling. Ask your doctor about using
a decongestant. Sauna and steam are also good for sinus
problems. While you were pregnant, you were probably told to
avoid hot rooms because they could raise your blood pressure.
Now it's good for you and your skin, but to be safe, have your
blood pressure checked before you go in.

> ### *Stay Off the Scale!*
> You've lost a lot of fluid since the birth, but probably not a lot of weight. So, again, don't head for the scale. If you are typical, you lost about 12 to 15 pounds in the hospital. Forget about dieting for at least a few weeks and eat a well-balanced diet. If you have too rapid a weight loss (which is unlikely), you will be more prone to keep the stretch marks on your breasts even if you lose the pounds.

Skeleton

While you were pregnant, your entire skeletal alignment changed. In order to carry the weight of the baby in front, your pelvic bones had to spread apart and tilt slightly. The distribution of weight on your knees and ankles was very different too. You're still not walking or even standing the way you used to. In 9 months, you figured out how to "waddle" so that your weight was over both femurs (thighbones). All of a sudden the weight is "gone," lying over there in the bassinet. Your skeleton will gradually shift back and your old posture will return.

Feet

Your feet may have grown and you may have gone up half a shoe size. Although they usually shrink after birth, they don't always, so don't buy shoes for at least three months.

Nutrition

New mothers still have specific nutritional needs. That's why most obstetricians recommend you continue to take your prenatal vitamins for the first 3 months after pregnancy, particularly if you are nursing, but even if you are not. You have just lost a large portion of your calcium, iron and basic minerals to the baby. You need to replenish your supply.

Plenty of Fluids

If you are a nursing mother, you will need to drink a lot of fluids. Make sure there's always a pitcher of something you like waiting in the refrigerator. Obviously drink the "right" kind of fluids, such as water and decaffeinated tea, and avoid salt-retaining liquids, such as fruit and vegetable juice. The bloated feeling they give you is as bad as being dehydrated. If you have waited 9 months to have a real cup of coffee, go for it, but in moderation.

The same advice holds for alcohol. I've had new mothers say, "I've been so good, can't I just have a glass of wine?" It's a tough call. I tell my new mothers: Never get intoxicated, but an occasional glass of wine with dinner will do no harm to the baby, and may do you some good.

Physical Activities

In many ways, you are limited in what you can physically do by your doctor, who probably advised you "don't do anything"—until your next visit. With the exception of heavy lifting and jumping, there are other physical activities you can enjoy. Just make sure to stop and listen to your body. You certainly can take walks. Just put baby in a Snugli® or other type of front carrier and march out the door.

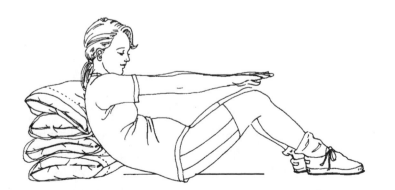

Exercise helps you return to your pre-pregnancy state.
Check with your doctor before beginning any exercise program.

> ### Caution
>
> This is not the time to start or go back to high- or even low-impact aerobic workouts. If you do, you may bleed heavily. In fact, women who go right back to work without giving themselves a few weeks off often have chronic bleeding that can last up to a year and lead to anemia and chronic malnutrition.

You need to strengthen your abdominal muscles. Every time you do something that requires lifting, such as picking up the baby, tuck in your stomach. This protects and strengthens your back muscles as well. Do tummy tucks, and keep doing the Kegel exercises you practiced during pregnancy.

Set aside some time for an exercise session. Do some stretching and relaxation exercises. If you had a vaginal delivery and were in good physical shape before you became pregnant, slowly add some sit-ups. There are also exercise tapes specifically designed for post-pregnancy. Rent them and try them out. As the days go by, take longer and longer walks. If you have access to a pool, you can get right back into the swim of physical activity.

If doing a certain activity—such as climbing stairs—hurts, then avoid the activity. The motto here should be, "No pain equals gain."

Driving

In general, you will be told not to drive for the first few weeks. The exception is if driving is the only way for you to go out and shop and no one else can be delegated to do this for you. Your blood loss can ebb and literally flow so keep a towel on the seat of the car. You could suddenly get woozy while driving. Pull off the road immediately if you are not feeling well. In addition, the sitting position that is necessary for driving may be the cause of some pain.

Mom at 6 Weeks

Although most mothers of 6-week-olds are still subject to the "blues," the physical toll has usually lessened. If you are breastfeeding, your breasts aren't as engorged. Your stitches have healed. Your episiotomy is tender but you are not afraid to have a bowel movement without a laxative. You can usually get in and out of the bathtub without assistance. You've been to your doctor by now.

Just a reminder: During your pregnancy, your doctor did many blood tests, including a measurement of your immunity to certain common illnesses. If you were not immune to rubella ("German measles") during your pregnancy, be sure your doctor gives you the vaccine now so that you and the baby will be safe from infection.

The blues may still be "playing" due to your fluctuating hormonal levels. You may, in fact, not experience a truly great day

---

When to Call Your Doctor

You will be seeing your obstetrician in 2 weeks, if you had a C-section, or in 4 weeks, if you had a vaginal delivery. Contact your doctor right away if you experience any of the following:

- Excessive bleeding (saturating a sanitary napkin every hour for more than 4 hours)

- Bleeding, with a foul-smelling odor

- Temperature of 101F/38.3C or above

- Shaking chills

- Constant lower abdominal pain

- A vein or area in your leg that feels sore and tender, or one leg swells more than the other

- A red, warm area on a sore breast

- Anxiety, depression or sleeplessness that is escalating

until your estrogen level begins to rise again. So don't be surprised if you still cry occasionally. As one new mom said, "Now that the baby is a few weeks old, I feel that I have *time* to cry." Be nice to yourself right now, until your old self catches up once again.

Part III

Tender Loving Care— Babies

Introduction

Now it's time for the daily nitty-gritty of baby care. You may have experienced an initial euphoria after having the baby—as if you were sprinkled with "pixie dust"—but soon it blows away and reality sets in. A new mother's work is never "done"—mothering is full-time, around the clock—with the rewards measured in smiles and coos!

There has been a lot of discussion of so-called *quality time,* but you can't have quality *without* quantity. It's important that you don't underestimate the importance of what you are doing. Tender loving care is just that. When you feed your baby, for example, you are also helping him to develop trust. When you give him a bath, you do more than clean him—you are loving him as well.

Don't underestimate the importance of what you are doing.

Just as you are learning to mother, your husband should be learning to father. (I jokingly tell new parents, "Your baby needs a 'mother' bath and a 'father' bath.") Fortunately, more and more dads are actively participating in the daily care of babies. (At a new shopping center, I smiled at the sign on the men's bathroom that read: Fathers' Changing Station.)

Of course, there are still those fathers who don't appreciate babies. As one dad told me, "I'll get more involved as soon as my son is a person." I told that father, "Your baby is not *about* to be a person. He's *already* a person, and you should get to know him."

As the days and weeks go by, you will no longer need the figurative equivalent of a crystal ball to predict your day; you'll have true, hands-on experience at mothering, and will know what to expect. You may know, for example, that by ten in the morning, your baby will have been fed, bathed, dressed and is ready for an outing. You'll also know that, despite all your best efforts, there will be those mornings when you're ready to go out but the baby's hungry, you feed him, he spits up, he needs a change of clothes, *you* need a change of clothes, he naps, and it's time to feed him once again. Eventually, however, you will start to develop routines you can generally rely upon. (You'll know, for example, that the diapering, feeding and rediapering routine seems to take anywhere from one to two hours.)

As the following chapters give you the basic facts you need to transform you from an amateur into an expert, don't be surprised if a friend who just had a baby now turns to *you* for advice!

5

Feeding

Feeding time is a wonderful opportunity to be close to your newborn. You get your baby's undivided attention. When the baby is in your arms and you are feeding her, you are where she can see you best. You hold her close and feed her, she looks into your eyes and she feels good. She associates the "yummy" sensations in her mouth with the warmth and love shown in your face. Feeding is the first step toward developing a trusting relationship with your baby.

Bottle versus Breast

Even before birth, mothers usually have made the decision about whether or not they want to breastfeed. It may be a gut decision. You either do or you don't want to breastfeed. Mothers rarely feel as strongly about whether to bottle-feed. The loaded emotional issues are tied to the decision to breastfeed.

Try clicking on these two Web sites for more information on breastfeeding versus bottle-feeding:

http://www.aafp.org/patientinfo/breastfd.html

http://www.fda.gov/opacom/catalog/breastfed.html

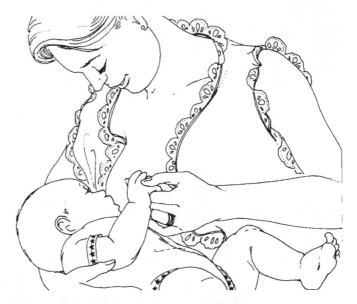

Feeding your baby should be a total experience involving smell, touch, and sight as well as good nutrition.

The Mother's Choice

Let me make my position clear. Although there are many wonderful advantages connected to breastfeeding, it is *not* the only way to adequately nourish your child. We now have the capability of feeding babies healthfully with formula.

I am in favor of breastfeeding for the woman who wants to. Sometimes a drug that a mother is taking or an illness that a mother has may keep her from breastfeeding. Anatomy rarely plays a part. I've seen the most amazing things happen when a woman is determined to breastfeed.

For example, women with inverted nipples are often advised not to breastfeed, or to use a special "shield" that can help create enough suction to get the breast milk flowing. I've seen women with inverted or flat nipples who, after a few days of suction pumping, found that their nipples "popped" out.

Breastfeeding

Advantages

❧ **"A perfect food."** Breast milk is ideally suited for babies' growth and development. (One of my mothers dubbed it the best "power breakfast.") It's nature's perfect product.

❧ **Wonderful immunological properties.** Breast milk has immunological properties that no other substance has. That is, it helps baby build up resistance to certain illnesses, from the common cold and ear infections to allergies. No one has been able to duplicate these properties exactly in formula. New research shows that nursing not only provides temporary protection against infection, but also it helps to trigger the baby's own immune system, because maternal

> Mothers often tell children, "Drink your milk, it's good for you." Nowhere is that more true than with breast milk.

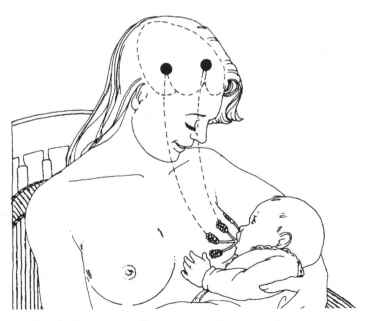

Your body is hormonally programmed to respond to your baby's hunger by providing nourishment.

immune factors are transferred through milk. (A protein component of breast milk activates certain white blood cells in the infant's body, causing them to develop sooner.) Another study found that breastfeeding has a preventive effect on urinary tract infections in both mother and infant.

- **Helps baby's digestive system.** Breast milk has a stimulating effect on a baby's bowel. It is also a natural stool softener, making it easier for the baby to pass the meconium—the dark and sticky first stools. Breastfed babies' stools are therefore generally soft and pass easily, often with every feed. Even if a mother breastfeeds for only a short time, it's still very helpful to the baby's developing digestive system.

- **A practical solution.** Breastfeeding is also practical. The milk is available, it's free, it's always at the right temperature, and it's there when you need it.

Disadvantages

- **Breastfed babies feed more often.** Breastfed babies are fed more often than bottle-fed babies. Many breastfeeding mothers must nurse about every 2 hours—or 12 times a day for the first few weeks. That's a lot of time spent feeding. Bottle-fed babies usually feed about 6 times per day or every 4 hours.

- **Breastfeeding takes time.** Not all babies have the same feeding style. Some feed like barracudas. Others are little gourmets. There are babies who can empty your breast in 5 minutes, while others take 20 minutes on just one side. There is no question it can be exhausting, but all this feeding also has a purpose. Breastfeeding keeps you attached to your baby—both literally and figuratively—at a time when you can barely contemplate doing much of anything else. Therefore, the mechanics of breastfeeding

> Not all women are comfortable breastfeeding outside of the privacy of their home. However, there are some cleverly designed clothes with strategically placed flaps, so that you can breastfeed unnoticed practically anywhere.

require a great deal of commitment in time and attention.

❥ **You might stay close to home.** For at least the first month of your baby's life, you are frequently unable to leave the house for more than 2 hours at a time, unless you plan to breastfeed outside.

> A news producer for *60 Minutes* told me that she was concerned about the whirring sound her breast pump made at work. However, her colleagues assumed she had a new high-power rewind button on her video recording equipment!

❥ **Work concerns.** There are additional concerns if you plan to go back to work and continue to nurse. How can you express breast milk at work without its interfering with work? Answer: With a little ingenuity. (See "Back to Work," pages 191 to 196, for advice on meeting the challenge of breastfeeding.)

❥ **Baby eats what you consume.** Everything you take into your body passes to some extent into the breast milk. Breastfeeding does force you to eat more healthfully, which is good, because the food you eat passes to baby as a breakdown product of that food. But you and your baby will also have to come to peace with this. Some foods, like chocolate, which has some caffeine in it, may be hard on baby and harder for you to give up than others. And if you have a cocktail, your infant is imbibing as well. Obviously any medicine you take, so does your baby. You will have to ask your doctor to clear each and every drug you take, both prescribed and over the counter. See the box on page 87 for guidelines on the nutritional needs of a breastfeeding woman.

❥ **Vitamins for mom may be recommended.** Breastfed babies may require more of some specific vitamins like A and D. Many

Also check the drpaula.com Web site for additional nutrition ideas for breastfeeding women:

http://drpaula.com/breastfeeding

mothers are themselves deficient in those vitamins and they don't pass well into breast milk. Most pediatricians routinely recommend breastfeeding mothers continue taking their prenatal vitamins.

Early Feeding

Most new mothers usually do not produce enough milk to express for at least a week. Conveniently, newborns aren't born hungry. Mother Nature has the breastfeeding system under control!

Colostrum

The earliest milk is called *colostrum* and it is produced in the last 3 weeks of pregnancy. First-time mothers usually don't produce even noticeable amounts of colostrum until at least the third day after the baby's birth.

Colostrum is special. *Colostrum* is immunologically different from the rest of the milk. It is richer in proteins and fat and is highest in immunoglobulins, which provide protection against a variety of illnesses.

Let Her Suck Often, but Not for Long

Put your baby to your breast often. It helps prime the hormonal pump. And you both will be rewarded. Your baby will have the opportunity to learn to suck, and you will gain by feeling close to your baby while your body is being stimulated to produce milk.

It is important, however, that you don't let her suck forever. Sucking on a "dry" breast may be pleasurable for you and the baby, but it's not good for your nipples. By day 3 or 4, when your breasts get engorged with milk, you will have painful, chapped, even bloody nipples. If you use your body as a human pacifier, to satisfy her sucking instincts, then when your milk does come in, your nipples will most likely be raw. Repositioning and getting more of the aereola into the baby's mouth also helps.

I suggest that in the first 2 or 3 days after your baby is born you attempt to put baby to your breast every 2 to 3 hours, or when baby wakes. Let her stay there for about 15 minutes on a side, regardless of whether you are yet producing milk.

When bottle-feeding, hold your baby in a semi-upright position to help keep air from being swallowed and to reduce the chances of ear infection.

*Find the positions that are most comfortable for you both—
lying on your side is often restful and comfortable.*

Lying with your baby head to tail can be a comfortable breastfeeding position.

Waking Baby

Don't slap baby's feet or pinch her skin to wake her. Undress your sleeping child completely and lay her on a flat surface, like the bed. That will usually startle her awake. Once she's up, nurse her while she is still naked except for a diaper. She's more likely to stay awake this way than if she's swaddled, cozy and warm, against your breast.

Colostrum also contains a protein, *lactoferon*, that helps the baby's body absorb iron to prevent anemia. Colostrum is a clear fluid and sometimes mothers think they are not making any milk when they see this fluid. Remember that regular milk does not come in until about the third or fourth day.

Baby loses weight at this time. Generally newborn babies eat next to nothing for a few days and are just fine. They are busy losing weight—about 5% of their birth weight in just the first week. However, this doesn't mean you shouldn't try to feed your baby. Just don't be surprised or upset if she sucks briefly and nothing comes out.

When Milk Comes In

Women have very different responses when the first-time milk does come in. It can be mildly uncomfortable or, as one mother said, "I could feel my fillings tingle."

When your breast milk first comes in, you may experience some pain as your breasts swell in size. If you briefly apply cold compresses, you will relieve some of the discomfort while also slowing the entry of milk. Warm compresses will increase the milk flow, and make you feel "worse." Once the swelling is reduced and a week or so has passed, you can use warm compresses or even a shower to encourage more milk flow— especially if tension is getting in the way of production.

Making Sure Baby Gets Enough

Be aware that some babies don't wake up very often the first week and may even be difficult to arouse. Although that may sound like a blessing, in fact, a few of these babies are actually a little dehydrated, especially if their room is dry or overheated.

How do you know if you are dealing with a dehydrated baby? In general, by the fourth day your baby should feed between 6 to 10 times or every 2 to 4 hours. If you have a baby who does not feed at least 6 times a day, consider waking her a little earlier to get in an extra feeding.

She should have several wet diapers a day. If diapers are wet before she falls asleep, everything is most likely fine. If, on the other hand, the baby's diapers are dry most of the day, contact your pediatrician and wake your baby to feed more often.

More Breastfeeding Information

For additional information about breastfeeding, visit these sites:

http://www.lalecheleague.org

http://drpaula.com/topics/breastfeed.html

Nipple Care

During those first few days, leave your blouse or robe open as often as you can so air and light will get to your nipples and they will begin to toughen up. To help toughen them, sit about 1 foot away from the warmth of a regular light bulb and fan the air toward your breast with your hands. This will help you to better withstand the pressure and suction of the baby's mouth when your milk is finally produced and your baby sucks.

I don't recommend putting ointments or gels on your nipples. They taste lousy when the baby does suck, and they are hard to wipe off without actually recracking and hurting your nipples.

Length of Feedings

Some breastfeeding specialists suggest you let the baby suck as long as she wants to. The reason for this is that the milk's immune properties increase in concentration as the length of the feedings increase. However, the richest milk—that is, the milk with the highest quantity of fat—is in the earliest part of the feed.

I'm firmly opposed to letting newborns nurse for as long as they want to. You will irritate your nipples, you will be exhausted, and you'll barely know where one feed ends and the next begins. Frustration and sheer exhaustion combine to cause many women to give up breastfeeding altogether, and they often feel guilty in the process.

Set limits. I suggest that after the third or fourth day you set yourself a goal of 15 minutes on each side, whether your baby is sucking actively or just "fooling around" on the breast. Try again at least every 3 hours unless baby demands more. Then set yourself a minimum limit of at least 1-1/2 hours from the start of one feed to the start of the next. This will insure your baby's getting plenty of nutrition while you are getting plenty of breaks from nursing.

Don't Offer Baby Water if You Breastfeed

If, before 1-1/2 hours from the last feed, your baby seems hungry again, give her one of three things: your finger, her finger, a pacifier. I *don't* recommend that you give the newborn baby a bottle of formula or water. If you want to fully establish breastfeeding, you don't want to give the baby any other liquid, because it may reduce the inspiration to breastfeed.

Except for the initial "trial run" right after birth (see page 20), I generally don't suggest using bottles of water unless there is a specific need—for example, dehydration or hard stools. If you give the baby water, which doesn't satisfy hunger, you are taking time away from breastfeeding. You could even make breastfeeding more difficult.

It's been suggested that baby could become confused between the rubber nipple and the maternal nipple. Babies don't really get confused, but they do go for what is easiest, and it takes less effort to suck out of a bottle than a breast.

Recommended Daily Allowances for Nursing Mother

Nutrient	Non-Pregnant Need	Pregnant Need	Nursing Need	Food Sources
Protein	46 g	75-100 g	66-70 g	Milk, cheese, eggs, meat, grains, legumes, nuts
Calories	2100	2400	2600	Carbohydrates, fats (200-300 calories per day during the first 3 months after birth come from the mother's stored fat)
Minerals				
Calcium	800 mg	1200 mg	2300 mg	Milk, cheese, grains, leafy vegetables, egg yolks
Phosphorous	800 mg	1200 mg	1200 mg	Milk, cheese, lean meats
Iron	18 mg	18 mg+30 mg-60 mg supplement	18 mg	Liver, other meats, eggs, grain, leafy vegetables, nuts, dried fruits
Iodine	100 mcg	125 mcg	150 mcg	Iodized salt, seafood
Magnesium	300 mg	450 mg	450 mg	Nuts, soybeans, cocoa, seafood, whole grains, dried peas
Vitamins				
A	4000 IU	5000 IU	6000 IU	Butter, cream, fortified margarine, green and yellow vegetables
D	0	400 IU	400 IU	Fortified milk, fortified margarine (and sunshine)
E	12 IU	15 IU	15 IU	Vegetable oils, leafy vegetables, cereal, meats, eggs, milk
C	45 mg	60 mg	80 mg	Citrus fruits, berries, melon, tomatoes, green vegetables, potatoes
Folic Acid	400 mcg	800 mcg	600 mcg	Liver, green vegetables
B complex				
Niacin	13 mg	15 mg	18 mg	Meat, peanuts, beans, peas
Riboflavin	1.2 mg	1.5 mg	1.9 mg	Milk, liver, grains
Thiamin	1.0 mg	1.3 mg	1.4 mg	Meat, grains
B_6	2 mg	2.5 mg	2.5 mg	Grains, liver, meat
B_{12}	3 mcg	4 mcg	4 mcg	Milk, eggs, meat, cheese

You should understand that your breasts never completely empty out like a bottle. In fact, you are constantly making milk, just not always in large quantities. It takes about an hour between feedings for your breasts to have enough milk to be pumpable again.

Baby's time on breast gradually lengthens. After 2 weeks or so, once the baby is latching on and sucking well, she can suck out about 90% of the milk in the first 5 minutes. Even at the beginning she is very efficient at feeding, taking 2 to 3 sucks and then dozing off. If she seems to still be hungry, switch back to the first side if she doesn't stop sucking.

When do you stop? I can answer that question with another question. For how long are you comfortable being attached to the baby? After the first few weeks, your nipples will be tough enough to handle even 20 minutes on a side.

Let Her Digest

Even a newborn baby needs time to digest. If you feed your baby for very long periods, with one feed beginning shortly after the last, you are inviting a baby version of indigestion and spitting up. When your baby stops feeding, a lot of digestive activity begins. If you could see into their little stomachs after eating, you'd witness many digestive enzymes pouring out to do their job. Let them do just that for a time.

Adding a Bottle

I recommend that even breastfeeding mothers consider introducing a bottle to the baby's routine after the first 2 to 3 weeks. By this time, a bottle of formula or a bottle of expressed breast milk could be used once a day or once every other day. (Pumped milk keeps 24 hours in the refrigerator and months in the freezer.)

The purpose of adding an occasional bottle to her daily menu is so she will not turn down a bottle if it is *necessary* to give her one. You are doing this for both you and your baby. Your baby will learn how to transfer her breastfeeding suck to the hard nipple version. And you will be reassured knowing if you have to leave the house your baby can still be fed.

I believe that all children should have the option of knowing how to suck and digest milk from a bottle for the purposes of survival. You may not always be available. If you don't try this rather early, your baby may reject your attempts later on.

Bottle-Feeding

Advantages

• If you are bottle-feeding, you feed your baby less often than breastfeeding moms—about six times a day. You will be less physically tied down to your baby and someone else can easily do the feeding.

• Your body should return to its prepregnancy state more quickly.

• Bottles are also handy because you can take them out anywhere and you can tell just how much the baby is getting.

How Much Will Baby Eat?

In the first 2 weeks, your baby may drink anywhere from 1/2 ounce to 4 ounces at each bottle-feed. Some babies benefit from the higher caloric content of formula, and may seem more satisfied than after breastfeeding. They tend to sleep for longer periods of time, and they may even gain weight a little faster.

> Never change the formula unless you have discussed the change with your doctor. There *are* differences. For example, soy-based formulas tend to constipate, while predigested formulas loosen stools. They are *not* interchangeable.

Formula

Modern formulas are otherwise quite similar to breast milk, in protein and carbohydrates. Most of today's formulas contain adequate amounts of vitamins. If your formula is a concentrate or powder, find out if fluoride is added to your local water supply. Too much fluoride can be a problem. Ask your doctor. (Some fluoride is good for your teeth.)

Myths

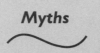

❧ *Myth:* **If you breastfeed, you lose weight.**

❧ *Myth:* **If you breastfeed, you don't lose weight.**

The truth is: You don't lose *or* gain weight because you are breastfeeding. Actually how you fare has to do with how much you actually eat, and not how much or often you nurse.

❧ *Myth:* **Breastfeeding is a form of birth control.**

This is definitely NOT true. It is not a reliable contraceptive method at all. There are women who don't have a menstrual flow while they are breastfeeding, but they can ovulate and therefore become pregnant.

❧ *Myth:* **You need to drink a lot of milk.**

Wrong. You don't need to drink milk to make milk, but you *do* need to drink a lot of fluids. Cows eat grass and they have no problem making milk.

❧ *Myth:* **Drinking beer or wine makes the milk richer.**

Current research proves this one is also wrong, though it has been passed down through the ages. If you are more relaxed, for whatever the reason, your milk will flow in larger but not richer quantities.

❧ *Myth:* **Women with big breasts have an easier time breastfeeding.**

Nothing could be further from the truth. The size of your breasts has no impact on how much milk you make. A new mother recently told me, "I failed to breastfeed with my first child, so I don't expect to do well this time. My breasts are too small." I explained that large breasts are filled with fat and not with more mammary ducts. You have adequate breast tissue no matter what size they are.

Common Questions

> **Q: I have a cold. Do I continue to breastfeed?**
>
> **A:** Yes, you have the advantage over bottle-feeding mothers in that your baby is not only exposed to your germs but also to your antibodies. While you have a cold, you are also fighting it by producing immunity, and it is transferred to your baby via your breast milk.

> **Q. Can I take a decongestant or other cold remedy?**
>
> **A.** Stick to home remedies—steam, tea and honey—to get over your cold. If you do take any medication, check it out with your doctor first. I've had to treat babies who developed side effects to over-the-counter cold pills taken by their nursing mothers.

> **Q: I have been waiting 9 months to have a permanent or dye my hair. Can I, now that my baby has been born?**
>
> **A:** It's not recommended that you have any chemical processes applied to your hair while you are still breastfeeding. Chemicals pass into your general body circulation and therefore get passed along to the baby as well.

> **Q: How can I tell if my baby is getting enough milk?**
>
> **A:** This is not easy to answer. Obviously there aren't any "ounce marks" on your breasts, the way there are on a bottle. If your baby is urinating and making stool, she is getting enough milk. (See chapter 10, *Baby's Health*.) Remember at the end of the first 2 weeks of life, all we expect is that the baby regain the ounces she lost and weighs in at her birth weight once again.

Disadvantages

- A major disadvantage is the way bottle-feeding makes some mothers feel. There is a sense that moms who "really care" breastfeed. By its title alone, a popular book called *The Womanly Art of Breastfeeding* could lead a mother who bottle-feeds to think she is somehow *"un*womanly."

- Some new mothers feel that if they bottle-feed they are depriving their baby of a bonding experience. We've all seen those beautiful pictures of nursing mothers. However, there is nothing to stop you from bottle-feeding while you are holding your semi-naked baby against your own naked chest. Fathers can do that as well and have the pleasure of skin-to-skin bonding.

> Interestingly, we know that babies have a sense of taste, but we don't know too much about it. They will sometimes spit out or refuse formula, so you may have to switch to one they prefer. There is also the slight risk of feeding baby spoiled formula, so always taste what you offer.

- Even though it is true that bottle-fed babies do not get the immune component in breast milk, whole generations of healthy babies have been reared on bottle-feedings.

- It's more expensive to bottle-feed, and you have to buy and stock up on the necessary supplies.

Getting Started

- Your baby will be offered prepared formula in the hospital. The formula the hospital uses is usually the one the doctor recommended. If your baby has problems digesting the formula—irritability, rashes, difficulty burping—you may need a change in formula.

- In general, bottle-feeding is easier today than it was for our mothers. It's no longer necessary to make your own formula, or to boil the water unless you live somewhere where the well water is not clean. We *do not* sterilize bottles anymore either. You don't even need to warm the bottles—room temperature is probably perfect—and even a cold bottle is fine at 3 in the morning. (Studies show that

> Some problems that arise with bottle-feeding are easy to fix. A mother came in with a crying baby. We discovered there was no hole in the nipple. Sometimes you have to make the hole.

the less time the baby is screaming and waiting for you to warm the bottle, the better all around.)

- The type of nipple the baby prefers often depends on what they are comfortable with from the beginning. There are orthodontic-shaped nipples, and there is reasonable evidence that they are easier for baby to suck milk from without getting air in. But there is no solid evidence that it makes any difference to the ultimate orthodontia of the baby. Most hospitals do start on "O" nipples, but any brand is fine. I prefer silicone because they are clear and less likely to disintegrate if accidentally overboiled, but they are often harder to find. Latex nipples are notable for breaking down and getting gummy, so keep extras on hand. (I don't want baby inadvertently munching on disintegrating plastic, which can happen when sticky and gooey latex nipples are boiled repeatedly.)

- I prefer clear plastic to glass bottles because of the possibility of glass shattering. The type of bottle you use is not as important as *how* it's held. Try not to let air get into the nipple.

- Always hold the bottle. Never prop it up. It's both physically and psychologically dangerous. Your baby could gag and choke. If you lay her down with her bottle and the bottle drops out of her mouth, she may experience both frustration and intestinal discomfort by sucking milk and air. It also lacks intimacy and is emotionally depriving. You are missing the opportunity for mother/baby eye contact and the relationship of trust that develops.

- If you are interrupted while feeding, take the bottle out of the baby's mouth, even if she cries.

More Bottle-Feeding Information
Try these Web sites for more bottle-feeding information:
http://www.playtexbaby.com/care-frm.htm
http://www.meadjohnson.com/products/cons-infant/enfaprof.html
http://www.similac.com
(Go to FEEDING YOUR BABY and click on CHOOSING TO FORMULA FEED.)

You can try several burping positions, but a burp is not always necessary.
If baby is happy and calm during feeding, spend no more than a
few minutes trying to "get the air out."

Getting Comfortable

When bottle-feeding, try sitting in a comfortable rocker or armchair and place pillows under your elbows. Cradle your baby close to your breast, with her head held a little higher than the rest of her body. Keep the bottle tipped so that air doesn't appear in the nipple.

If you have twins, feed them individually or lay both down on a soft pillow and hold one bottle in each hand. I have four sets of triplets in my practice. They are fed in round-robin fashion—two get to feed, and one gets to watch.

Burping

All babies need to be burped. Burp a bottle-fed newborn after every ounce of formula. Stop between breasts to burp a breastfed baby. Just put baby over your shoulder and pat firmly, in the middle of her back, not near the top of the chest. Give up after 5 minutes. Most babies burp spontaneously if you lay them down. Put a little pressure on their back and you may find a little

Burp a bottle-fed newborn after every ounce of formula.

Another comfortable position that helps baby to burp or pass gas is with the baby lying across your lap.

This is another good burping position, in which the baby sits upright on your lap while you pat firmly on the middle of her back.

spit-up appears under their cheek. You may also produce a burp. If you put your baby in an infant-feeding seat, her inclined posture may also aid digestion.

Growth Spurts

Babies tend to grow in sudden spurts and not gradually. At about three weeks and again at six weeks, when these spurts are likely to occur, you may notice that both bottle- and breastfed babies start to feed voraciously. This is not commonly known and just about every mother in my practice calls me to discuss her suddenly ravenous baby.

If you are bottle-feeding, let your baby take the lead. She really won't take too much, and even if she did, she would eventually spit up, which would cause no harm.

If you are breastfeeding, go back to feeding every 2 hours. In a short amount of time your breasts will have more milk per feeding.

This may be the month the baby will gain 2-1/2 pounds instead of 1. The typical baby gains 4 to 8 ounces a week. Breastfed babies gain about 1 pound a month. Bottle-fed babies gain a little more. You want the baby to have doubled her birth weight by 6 months, although many bottle-fed babies double their birth weight sooner.

For more about growth spurts, try this Web site:

http://www.drpaula.com/topics/growth.html

On Demand or On Schedule?

I suggest you feed your newborn when she cries and nothing else will soothe her. With few exceptions, feed the baby when she's hungry.

Supply and Demand

In order for the quantity of breast milk to increase to meet the needs of your growing baby, there must be times when your baby feeds voraciously and frequently. This doesn't mean you don't have enough milk. Your baby's vigorous sucking is a signal to the mammary glands to produce more milk and then feeding frequency will slow up again, because there will be more milk available *per feeding*. This is a true supply/demand system.

Adding a formula bottle at this time is exactly what *not* to do if you want to continue to breastfeed exclusively. After a few days, and within a week at the most, the baby should settle down again to feeding every 3 to 4 hours.

If you are the kind of person who likes to follow a schedule, to some extent you may succeed in imposing a feeding routine on your baby, but it won't be as predictable as you'd like. In fact, it shouldn't be rigid, because you can't expect your baby to suppress her appetite or to eat when she's not hungry just because four hours have passed.

On the other hand, if you want the baby to tell you when to feed her, you have to be sensitive to her signals of hunger. It's not always easy to tell, since most of what babies do at this age is cry. Sticking a nipple in your baby's mouth every time she cries will at least temporarily satisfy most needs other than pain. But not every cry is a cry for food. (See chapter 7, *The Crying Baby*.) You don't want to teach her that eating is the solution to all of life's discomforts.

Here's a Good Rule of Thumb:

If your baby has been well fed within the past 1-1/2 hours, you can assume you are *not* dealing with a hungry baby.

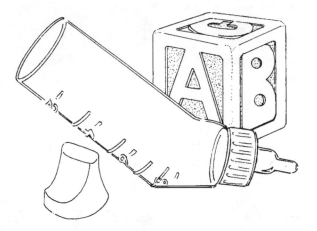

Use bottles that are designed to reduce the amount of air the baby can swallow.

Some people believe if you give formula late in the evening, your baby will sleep through the night. Sorry. There's no link between sleeping through the night and adding a late formula feeding. I advise parents not to be hemmed in by the need for consistency. (As I remind parents, "Consistency is the hobgoblin of small minds.") Babies don't mind if one day you give the formula feeding at 2 in the afternoon and next day at 2 in the morning.

If your baby is sleeping, unless you have specific instructions from the doctor (maybe baby was premature or underweight), *never wake a sleeping baby.* If you're lucky enough to have a baby who sleeps 5 hours through the night, just smile. And get some sleep!

Gas

What Causes the Gas?

Babies have gas from day one, but to differing degrees. Not all babies have pain. Some just produce gas painlessly though often noisily. The cause of it is the establishment of normal bacteria in your baby's gut (see box on opposite page).

Babies Don't Come Sterilized

I believe that the old notion of boiling bottles is nonsense. We are not sterile to begin with. If we were, we could not digest our food properly. Our intestines need to maintain a symbiotic relationship with normal bacteria. These bacteria participate in the process of digestion and produce gas. Pain is caused when gas expands and the intestines are stretched.

There is a period of adjustment to the various kinds of bacteria vying to set up shop in the proper proportions—just enough e. *coli*, just enough *enterococcus*, and so forth. In that battle, there are bound to be periods of distress.

Other causes of gas production are not so good. Some bottle-fed babies are plagued by gas as a result of maldigestion of milk. Most common formulas are based on cow milk, which contains a sugar and a protein that not all people can handle. Many adults, in fact, have intolerance to the sugar, called *lactose*, in cow's milk. In addition, when you pass undigested lactose into the lower intestine, it's very gas-producing. Sometimes it is necessary to switch baby's formula. Breastfed babies also have gas, but usually to a lesser degree.

How to Help Make Baby More Comfortable

You can help your baby deal with painful gas, which usually lasts for only a few seconds or minutes, in several ways. If it comes on rather frequently, then bowel distention is probably causing the pain. The gas is "stuck." You can actually hear the gut rumbling and see the baby kicking.

Put baby in motion: into an infant seat, swing, sling or a stroller rocked back and forth. Even just hoisting the baby up on your shoulder may help, because gas moves and will, with motion and gravity, "fall" in one direction or the other.

Some kinds of teas may absorb or help break up the gas.

Or you could put baby belly-down on a hard surface with a soft covering, and rock her from side to side while putting some pressure on her back with the palm of your hand. Flattening her belly helps to roll the gas along.

According to folklore, feeding certain kinds of teas, such as chamomile, anise or fennel, to your baby also works well. The teas absorb or break up the gas. Brew a weak solution using equal parts tea and cold tap water.

There are a series of drugs on the market for treating gas that are simethecone-based. I don't recommend them because they rarely work and they can sedate the baby unnaturally.

The Psychology of Feeding: Including Father

There is little that bonds a relationship more than having the responsibility for another person's sustenance. Feeding is supportive in the most basic way. It's not uncommon for fathers to feel left out of the incredibly intense relationship that is evolving between mother and baby, even when the mother is bottle-feeding.

It's not just nursing mothers who exclude fathers, but certainly breastfeeding accentuates the issue. The husband may

It's important to share the feeding and bonding experience.

look longingly at his wife, whose breasts no longer seem to "belong" to him, and at his baby, who doesn't seem to need him much either.

It's also often uncomfortable for most women to resume sexual relations with their husbands while they are breastfeeding. Their breasts are leaking milk and often hurt. All of this may delay husband and wife becoming a couple again. And now there appears to be a new couple in the house—mom and baby.

In general, there are two reasons why mothers have problems sharing the feeding—particularly breastfeeding mothers.

1. Some women have heard if they use a relief bottle of any sort the baby will have nipple confusion. That is, she will be confused between the action needed to suck on a breast nipple and the action needed to suck on a rubber nipple. The truth is, very little confusion actually occurs as long as you don't switch back and forth repeatedly. If a bottle is offered only once a day, or you've already established breastfeeding over the first two or three weeks, there is usually no problem. I can't recall a case of true nipple confusion under these conditions. Obviously, if you are bottle-feeding, there is no confusion at all.

2. Many new mothers don't want to lose control of the nurturing experience. This second reason strikes right at the heart of the matter. Breastfeeding mothers are not bonded any closer to their babies than bottle-feeding mothers, but they often believe that breast milk is superior and it's something only they can really do. I've heard mothers say with pride, "My baby wants nothing but me." It's a badge of honor some mothers wear: "Nothing has passed her lips except breast milk." This can easily cause fathers to withdraw and even fade out of the immediate picture. As one dad in a new-father's group lamented, "I don't have breasts. What can I do?"

Nipple confusion isn't usually a problem.

There is a device that allows fathers practically to breastfeed. It's a bra with two sacks and nipples on the end. After filling it with milk, the father slips on the device and he can "breastfeed." I personally think this is carrying things a little too far, but there are fathers who say it has helped them feel part of the experience.

Bottle-feeding mothers are often possessive. It's as if they think the hand that holds the bottle "owns" the baby! Some moms feel they have learned all of the tricks of the bottle-feeding trade and are a little jealous if dad too easily steps right in and succeeds.

Find a Role for Dad

Fathers should be encouraged to participate in feeding in a meaningful way. In the past, fathers used to be the person who fed the baby a bottle in the middle of the night. Breastfeeding mothers may let their husbands feed baby a bottle of pumped breast milk at that late hour.

I find that there is something very illogical and unfair about that. It's not quite right to expect your husband to happily bond at 2 A.M. when *he* is likely to be as exhausted as you are. You are really tossing him the crumbs of feeding by giving him the least desirable time.

Make a place for your partner in baby's feeding.

I suggest that new mothers understand that fathers also get to bond when they get to feed. Letting him feed the baby is an important step to bringing your threesome together and closing the gaps between you and your mate. Make a place for him. Now.

Hold mom and baby. Father can participate in feeding, even if the mother wants to breastfeed exclusively and is really uncomfortable with adding a bottle. One lovely way is for the father to hold his wife while she feeds the baby. Often it's in bed, usually late in the evening or early in the morning. Make it cozy and meaningful. This can be very rewarding if you are willing to let your partner be a part of it.

Let him do it his way. If your husband does feed the baby, then you have to let him do it his way. Some mothers feel they are the experts, the professionals, and the husband is sort of an amateur. Yes, it is difficult to watch someone who appears inept, who fumbles around with a bottle, so that maybe milk even slurps down baby's chin. The temptation is to step in and say, "No, honey, do it this way," or "Let me do it." Resist this and let the father and baby fumble on their own a little bit. They will work it out if you let them.

Special bonding opportunity. We know that a very special relationship does develop between the baby and the person who feeds her. During the first 3 months, baby can see most clearly at the distance from your arms to your eyes. That's what goes on during feeding. There is eye contact between baby and her feeder. It makes for memories of early love, and it's truly sad when father misses out on these moments. Later on, you'll be rewarded by the close relationship between father and child. Studies show that fathers who feed their babies play with them more as well.

Fathers can make memories of early love by feeding baby.

Coming Attractions

Both formula and breast milk will meet all of your baby's nutritional needs until at least 4 months and usually until 6 months. (At this age, babies go longer periods without eating.) For several good reasons, we no longer feed babies any solid food in the first few months.

In the past, mothers were advised to add cereal or fruit in a puréed form and just widened the nipple to accommodate it in the bottle. We were sneaking in extra calories. We now know that obesity has roots in early overfeeding. Worse, these foods just aren't meant to be eaten by a baby who can't sit up. The process of digestion isn't ready yet, and sucking coordination is not in place. The ability to gum, swallow and digest cereal or carrots kicks in at between 4 and 6 months.

Obesity has roots in early overfeeding.

Also, before that time, the body recognizes these foods as foreign and may develop antibody responses. The result is a variety of allergies and an allergic skin condition called *eczema*. Juice is not as good as the fruit it came from and should be avoided because it adds useless, sugary calories and may even harm the growing baby teeth.

When to Stop

If you are breastfeeding, you may have questions about when to stop. This is a personal issue. Your body will respond to demand for at least the first 5 to 6 months. In very few cases does the natural cycle of breastfeeding start to turn itself off earlier.

There are many ways to part-wean, particularly if you want to go back to work. Remember that greater than 80% of immunity is transferred to the baby in the first 3 months, so that this is often the time when mothers do choose to wean. However, breastfeeding even beyond the first year is more and more common and very satisfying to both baby and mom.

6

sleeping

A mother recently came into my office and showed me a card she had received congratulating her on the birth of her son. It read: "I know you will be able to rise to the occasion . . . about eight times a night." She was much too tired to laugh.

The truth is, the card was right on target. Sleepless nights and infants are a fact of most new parents' lives. So when this new mom asked me (as hundreds of mothers have before her), "How do I get my 3-week-old son to sleep through the night?" I answered, "You can't." What you can expect is to be up 2 to 4 times a night.

Sleeping Patterns

Infants don't sleep through the night the way adults do. They may sleep as many as 18 hours per day, but they do it in small bursts. All of us are capable of waking up many times during the night, yet we do so rarely. Our brain waves take us in and out of different levels of consciousness, sleep being one of those levels. Babies generally go through the same phases but more frequently.

Every 3 to 4 hours they alternate between sleeping lightly, deeply, lightly, deeply. On some of these occasions, they will become aware of the sensation of hunger, wake up fully, cry, and get fed. Then they sleep lightly, deeply, lightly, deeply again. This pattern repeats itself some 6 to 10 times a day.

For soothing lullabies, try my book, *365 Ways to Get Your Child to Sleep*, written with Linda Lee Small.

Day and Night

Babies also do not respond the same way adults do to darkness and light. Research shows that light responsiveness starts at about 5 to 6 months of age. Newborns can sleep in bright light and be wide-awake in the dark. I'll get frantic calls from a mother: "My baby is all mixed up. He doesn't know night from day and seems to sleep more during the day and less at night." The baby *isn't* confused and is unlikely to turn into a permanent night owl. He is just following his own time clock, which is different than ours.

Night and day are not distinguishable for a newborn. You can't fool a newborn into thinking it's night and time to go to sleep. You just have to live with it, and sleep when your baby sleeps. Most new mothers have no problem falling asleep if only they allow themselves to. Similarly, just as they can sleep in light, babies can usually sleep in a noisy environment. You don't need to whisper. You can usually safely assume that baby's sleep is independent of the noise level around him.

> ### The Eat-and-Sleep Myth
>
> It's a myth that giving a baby cereal in his bottle at night will fill him up and keep him down, or that a breastfeeding mother who drinks wine will lull the baby into a lengthier sleep. I say, to the former, cereal can cause indigestion and lead to more sleep problems. To the latter, wine can actually agitate babies.

Babies don't have sleep problems. Their parents do. There is no good reason for infants to sleep straight through the night except to have happier parents in the morning. In the pursuit of this happiness, tired moms have been known to try just about anything.

*Try to rest when your baby is sleeping, making sure
you are lying in a secure position.*

There's probably no topic that hits a nerve quite like babies
and sleeping. We can make jokes about it, as the greeting card
did, but there is just no getting around it: Your baby needs you
when he wakes up but at the same time you need your sleep.
Your newborn will not sleep through the night and neither will
you. For most adults, sleep deprivation is almost crippling.
(Just ask any medical intern or resident.) Many moms tell me it
makes them weep with frustration and dad absolutely has to do
some night patrol.

Unfortunately, there are no shortcuts to lengthening your
infants' sleeping sessions at this early age. Newborns don't
have the capacity to take in large quantities of food. They need
nourishment at regular intervals around the clock. If you
happen to have one of those rare newborns who does sleep
for long periods, your doctor may advise you to wake him to
feed—particularly if he was premature or if his weight gain
is insufficient.

> **Strong Warning**
>
> Do not leave the bottle in your baby's mouth after he falls asleep. You don't want him to become accustomed to drinking while sleeping. It's also dangerous, since he may choke. And it can lead to tooth decay.

Some good news is that breastfed babies tend to fall asleep easily after feeding. In fact, many fall asleep *while* they are feeding. The bad news is that they wake up about every 2 to 3 hours because they are hungry again.

On the other hand, bottle-fed babies can take in a larger load of calories per ounce of milk (breast milk has slightly fewer calories per ounce) and frequently sleep about 3 to 4 hours at a time.

Safe Sleep Positions

No perfect position. The American Academy of Pediatrics, citing research on SIDS (sudden infant death syndrome) prevention, released a statement that said that babies should not be placed on their bellies to sleep. There is a concern that you might place your baby on a soft surface and his face could sink in and obstruct breathing.

It's been my experience that the optimum position is on his side, because it is also difficult for many babies to remain asleep very long on their backs before being jarred awake by their own startle reflex. Provided the baby is on a firm surface, side lying is the position that most closely approximates the womb—knees up, neck flexed and arms tucked in.

To read the American Academy of Pediatrics research report on baby sleeping position and SIDS, go to the following address on the Web:

http://www.aap.org/policy/re9946.html

Baby's Bedroom

During the first few weeks of baby's life, it's probably safest and most convenient to have the baby sleep very close to you. Your baby wakes often, and it's easier to get him from the side of the bed than from the next room. It makes the most sense to put your newborn in a bassinet, cradle or even a carriage next to your bed when you get home from the hospital.

It's safe and convenient to have the baby sleep close by.

The bassinet should be small enough so that baby feels securely surrounded, yet large enough so when he stretches his arms they do not hit the sides. The typical bassinet is 18 inches across and 30 inches in length. Baby is approximately 20 inches long or 25 inches with his arms stretched up. By the time the baby is about two months old, he should be out of a bassinet and into a crib. Some babies turn over at 3 months and would be in danger of flipping out of a bassinet.

Mattress

Finding the right mattress for baby may sound a little bit like replaying "Goldilocks." This one may be too hard, that one too soft and finally you'll find the one that is *just right*. The mattress doesn't have to be hard and stiff, just firm enough so baby can't sink into it.

There can be a problem with homemade and makeshift sleeping areas. For example, some parents create sleep areas by placing a pillow inside an enclosed playpen. Unfortunately, the softness of the pillow might enable the baby's head to sink into it and create a pocket in which the baby could suffocate. Make sure the mattress isn't made of animal hair, because some babies will have an allergic reaction to it.

Bedding

Put a cotton sheet on the mattress and make sure it fits snugly. Most babies are not allergic to cotton and it seems to be more comfortable for them. Babies don't need pillows, even though pillows are included in blanket sets. If your baby sleeps on a pillow, he may bend his neck in a way that could make it harder for him to breathe freely. You can, however, have baby bumpers if they are narrow and secured tightly to the sides of the crib.

> The baby should have only pleasant associations with his crib. Don't ever use the crib as a "jail" or put him in it as an angry or punishing gesture. The crib will be your and baby's friend for the first two years. Don't transform it into an enemy.

The surface baby sleeps on should be free of all snaps, buttons and zippers. Every night, check the crib for anything that could have fallen in. Babies tend to grasp whatever is there and pull it right to their mouths. Blankets, when necessary, should be lightweight. In general, your baby's sleep outfit should be his blanket, not a heavy cover that he might get tangled in.

Developing Healthful Sleep Habits

For the first few weeks, nothing is more reassuring to the baby than physical contact. But after that, it is time to think of separating from him just as he is about to fall into deep sleep. I've heard mothers in my new-mother's groups complain, "Now what do I do? I've finally got the baby to sleep and I can't move!" When I ask, "Why?" they answer, "Because I'm under the baby."

Babies eventually learn to put themselves to sleep.

(Yes, you should try to sleep when the baby is asleep, but not necessarily while attached to each other!)

If you help your baby fall asleep in his bassinet or crib, he will be able to do it on his own much sooner. Your baby can eventually learn to put himself to sleep, but you can't expect him to go "cold turkey" from rocking on your nice warm body to just being put down in a crib still awake. When the baby is starting to fall asleep—his eyelids are fluttering—carry him to his crib before he is fast asleep.

> ### Tip
>
> If you use a pacifier to put your child to sleep, remember to remove it once he's nodded off. Again, don't get into the dangerous habit of giving your baby a bottle in his crib. Not only will he look for the bottle each time he wakens, but we now know that it can harm baby's teeth and he can choke on the fluid held in his mouth.

When you put him down in his crib, the last thing he remembers before falling asleep will be the first thing he searches for during the night when his sleep waves lighten. If that last thing was your arms or a bottle in his mouth and he can't easily replace it, he will invariably cry. What you would like him to be remembering is the nice, comfortable mattress.

After a few weeks, if he is still sleeping next to you in your room, you increase the chances of waking your baby. You tend to sleep lightly as a new parent. Every movement the baby makes wakes you and makes you think, "My baby is up, I should be up." No, you shouldn't. You will tend to feed each other's alert mechanisms.

Here's a common scenario: The baby makes a little noise. You lean over to see him and rustle the sheets. He wakes up and cries. Instead, I suggest you lie still when you hear that little noise and he will probably go right back to sleep. It's not fair to wake him at his first movement.

Sleep Tips

- If your baby is very jittery and has trouble sleeping, try swaddling him (see box on *How to Swaddle a Baby,* page 112). Sometimes being wrapped up snugly encourages baby to relax and sleep.
- It's nice to have a mobile, music or maybe one of the specially designed stuffed animals that simulate "uterine" ("womb") sounds.

> ### How to Swaddle a Baby
> 1. Turn one corner of a baby blanket down, off center.
> 2. Put your baby on the blanket a little to one side.
> 3. Wrap the shorter end around his body.
> 4. Fold the bottom corner up.
> 5. Now take the long end and wrap it all the way around him.

❧ Try holding a cloth diaper while you are nursing or feeding, and then put that cloth diaper in the crib along with baby. The smell the cloth acquires from your body, plus the association of it being there in your arms, is sometimes enough to make baby sleep. (See chapter 7, *The Crying Baby*, for more on transitional objects.)

❧ If baby doesn't sleep easily during the day, put him down for *little* catnaps on your belly. Or baby can even sleep in a Snugli front carrier. This way at least your hands are free and baby loves the motion. You can try a swing, as long as you are in attendance at all times.

❧ You can create a warm, cozy nap place by using a hot water bottle that is well wrapped in insulted material such as terry cloth. Fill it 3/4 full with lukewarm water. Put the baby on his side and mold the water bottle to his belly. It gives a nice sensation of warmth and motion and can even be helpful in other circumstances. (See "Gas," page 122, and "Colic," page 123.)

❧ It's important to remember that at this age your baby should *not* be left in his crib to cry. If he can't fall asleep after about five minutes, then he belongs back in your arms.

Napping

One of the ways baby passes his time is napping. Napping doesn't have to occur in the traditional sleeping-at-night position in his crib. It can occur anywhere. You may even be lucky enough to have a baby who naps when you go out for a walk.

Rocking

One way to help your baby to nap is to put him in a cradle.
I know they are not in vogue right now, but I've always liked
cradles. You already have a cradle, if you
think about it. You have your arms. There is   *Put your baby in*
no reason, in the first few months and   *a cradle to help*
especially during the day, why you can't sit   *him nap.*
in a rocking chair with baby napping on
you. Baby can even rock himself into a nap
in a rocking infant-feeding seat. Baby's slightest motion causes
more motion. You could also put the baby down for a nap in his
stroller and push it back and forth over a doorjamb. Today most
strollers have their own spring action for this purpose.

Catnaps

You can expect your newborn to spend many periods a day
"catnapping." These periods can range from 10 minutes to as long
as 2 hours. Some babies eat, are alert, then get irritable and
maybe eat again, and finally sleep for a short while. Sometimes
there are 1 or 2 periods a day when they sleep for 2 to 3 hours,
and then they may not nap at all.

As baby gets older, sleep will begin to normalize. Some
babies will nap briefly twice a day, while others take just one long
nap. It's common for babies to take one nap in the morning and
then an afternoon siesta and finally sleep through the night once
they reach 4 to 6 months.

Coming Attractions

The biggest changes in baby's sleeping patterns will occur at
about five months, or when the infant has doubled his birth
weight. It is no longer necessary to feed the baby in the middle of
the night. In addition, his sleep/wake brainwave patterns are such
that he doesn't waken as easily and he can now sleep for
increasingly longer periods.

If you follow these suggestions, you should be able to help
your baby sleep through the night:

A wise mother sleeps when her baby sleeps. It's also a wonderful opportunity to feel close to your newborn.

❧ You can't put your baby in his crib and expect him just to give up waking for sleeping. You need to let the baby *know* that it's bedtime. You might dim the lights, pull the shades and generally quiet the house. Some babies at 5 to 6 months do need pitch dark, and you may have to buy blackout shades for early morning sunlight. You are sending a message that it's now sleeptime. You might try saying out loud, "Now we're going to sleep, little one."

❧ You may want to develop a bedtime ritual that is different from naptime. Have a firm idea in your mind of how long it should last. Babies can tune into your vibrations. If you don't have an endpoint to the ritual, your baby won't have an endpoint, either. The ritual might be two lullabies, one cuddle-kiss and a trip around the room saying good night to the various stuffed animals and dolls. After a

You may want to develop a bedtime ritual.

while, your baby will come to expect that ritual. Do it over and over. Don't worry. Your baby won't get bored.

➤ When the ritual is over, put baby in his crib and rub or pat his back for a few moments. Turn on a lullaby tape, wind a musical mobile—anything baby likes to listen to. Or maybe just turn a favorite picture toward baby to look at as he closes his eyes. Remember it's hard for baby just to let go of you, so don't be surprised if he whimpers or whines a little.

It's perfectly normal for him to experience a little bit of distress as he gives up being awake. To a baby, this represents the ultimate separation from you.

I don't believe in letting a baby cry endlessly.

➤ If your baby continues to cry, wait 5 to 10 minutes, the time it should take for your baby to fall asleep. Ten minutes is about as long as your newborn can keep his image of you in his head without really panicking. This is also about as long as most parents can reasonably be expected to tolerate the noise. If the crying doesn't stop, then you need to return to the room at about 10-minute intervals. I don't believe in letting a baby cry endlessly.

➤ One popular childcare book advocates that parents wait increasingly longer periods to check up on baby. This usually makes the baby scream louder and longer because that will increase the chances of your coming back. I have had parents who followed that advice tell me that police have appeared at their door in the middle of the night because neighbors feared for the safety of the baby!

If you do go back in, less is best. Say almost nothing.

➤ If you do go back in, less is best. Say almost nothing. ("Shh. Go back to sleep.") Briefly reassure the baby you are there. Don't give him a bottle, and never pick up baby unless you want him to get up. (Maybe your husband just got home and hasn't seen the baby.) If you reward the baby for waking up by playing with him, he has no good reason to go back to sleep. As long as the baby continues to cry, you continue to check in at 10-minute intervals.

What if your baby goes easily to bed at 8:00 P.M., but then wakes up at 2:00 A.M.? Simple. You are back at the same place you would be if he had trouble going to sleep. Again, do as little as possible when you enter the room. If you don't reinforce his waking up, he can be taught to go back to sleep.

It should take about a week to get a 5- to 6-month-old baby to adapt to a more adult sleeping pattern and to be convinced that going to sleep and staying asleep can be a pleasant experience.

7

The Crying Baby

Except for the very first cry baby makes when she is born, there is no question that the sound of a baby crying seems to pierce right through your body. A new mom recently said, "Dr. Paula, I feel like I'm supposed to be able to 'read' Sam and know what he wants when he cries." But babies aren't such open books. It would be wonderful if infants were delivered with translation books to interpret their cries!

New mothers may think that they are supposed to know automatically what each cry means. No one can. At conventions, pediatricians have been asked to listen to tapes of crying babies, and they can't guess what the baby wants anymore than you can. The bottom line is that your baby has virtually no other way of communicating except through her cry.

How Babies Talk

Babies do talk, if you can understand their language. I like to think that babies are born singing. You and your baby form a "duet" from the moment of birth. At the very beginning, some mothers respond to their baby's voice by repeating, mimicking the sound, and baby usually responds to this "conversation" by repeating the sound back. Other mothers try to interpret the baby's sound—maybe it's a cry of hunger or distress—and respond not with a sound but with an action.

An Invisible Cord between Mother and Child

There are definite connections between our babies and our bodies. Again, there is that invisible cord. Within hours of birth, some mothers can even distinguish their own baby's cry from that of other babies.

It's been observed that breastfeeding mothers will produce more milk to the cries of their own baby, although they can produce milk to the cries of other babies as well. When babies cry, it's a communication meant just for you.

Volume

A newborn baby's cry varies mostly in volume. They have little control over the pitch or tone until about 2 to 3 months. Some babies are equipped with highpitched cries that many adults find irritating. As you might expect, the bigger the newborn, the louder the cry. Preemies have a very quiet cry. They literally don't have the strength to generate much volume.

Why Babies Cry

Babies cry for a variety of reasons, but it is always an expression of some need. They can be hungry, tired, wet, sick, uncomfortable, frightened, even lonely.

> Whenever I ask parents, "Why are you feeding the baby all the time?" the answer I get back is, "Because the baby is crying and she stops when I feed her." That may be true, but it doesn't mean the baby was hungry.

A common mistake parents make is to assume that every time baby cries, she must be hungry. They are too quick to respond with a feeding. I recently had a new mother tearfully complain to me that she feels as if she's become a kind of living bottle, nursing baby nonstop. This grown woman has allowed herself to be held hostage by a 7-pound crying baby.

The Case Against Monitors

I tell new mothers: Don't worry, you will definitely be able to hear your baby when she cries. That is why I *don't* recommend baby monitors. Unless you live in a very large house, monitors are unnecessary and can even be intrusive. Over the years, I've observed that a woman who was once a sound sleeper will wake at the slightest stir after she becomes a mother. There are good reasons why monitors are a bad idea. The monitor alerts you too quickly to the subtle, small sounds a baby makes (for example, rolling from side to side, stretching, rubbing against the sheets). Through a monitor, even a little sigh is transformed into a big cry.

I'm not trying to discourage mothers from responding to their babies, but not every sound a baby makes is a sound of distress. Your baby is learning that she has a voice and she needs to exercise it privately. If you respond too quickly to every sound she makes, she will have no opportunity to figure out what sounds she *can* make. Don't run in at every amplified whisper. It startles her if you dash in every time she makes a peep.

Monitors also create a false sense of security. It is as if the monitor is really standing guard over your baby. By mistakenly believing that you will be alerted if anything is wrong, you may not go in every once in a while just to check on baby. I tell new parents it's better to peek in occasionally, if that makes you feel better, than it is to hover over the microphone of the monitor.

Setting Limits

Right then and there I talked to the constantly nursing mother, as I've talked to countless other parents, about setting limits. Many mothers express the view that if they could anticipate every need their child had and prevent their child from feeling any discomfort, they would. Well, I wouldn't. You will be permanently doomed to failure if you try. And it's not even good for your baby. She is a growing, independent human being who deserves the right to learn how to communicate her needs.

We mistakenly feel if we only know what every cry means we will be able to create better, happier people. But even happy, healthy adults cry and feel discomfort and pain.

So the mother who is feeding her child all the time must develop a new dialogue in her head to replace the old one. For example: "It's not likely my child is hungry again after feeding well only 20 minutes ago. So I'll set a limit in my mind. For at least an hour, I'll try not to feed her again. I will try to figure out what else I can do to comfort her."

With this effort, you are teaching the baby a very important lesson. She is half of a communicating team. The baby holds some of the responsibility, though a limited one. You are both trying to understand each other, and you each have to expend some effort. Although they don't carry on the sophisticated internal dialogue of the adorable baby in *Look Who's Talking*, babies *can* communicate. They learn very quickly, for example, that crying brings certain results. What a wonderful lesson!

When Not to Set Limits

It's equally important to understand when *not* to set limits. Up to about three months, you do have to respond quickly to a crying baby. (But remember that "respond" doesn't always mean "feed.") You should pick up the baby. Some babies stop crying when they see an adult smile or when they are held very close. Feeling your touch, smelling your perfume, hearing you sing, listening as you wind up her mobile—all of those can quiet a crying baby. A baby who isn't attended to when she cries just cries more, not less. And most parents find it more painful to listen to the crying than to pick up the baby who can't really tell you what's bothering her.

> If grandma complains that you're going to spoil the baby by attending to her cries, answer, "Fruit spoils, not infants."

Again, research indicates that babies who cry and are picked up, cry less on the average then babies who are left to cry. As your baby grows a little older, about the third month, you can set small limits. From the open doorway of her room you reassure her, "Don't worry, Jenny, I'll be there in a minute." Jenny hears your voice, knows you are there, and calms down a little.

Communicate

When you do pick up your baby, always talk to her. The sooner you use language, the sooner you are coupling the feeling of comfort with the sound of comfort. ("Mommy is here.") Babies learn self-control by experiencing small doses of frustration. The goal of this particular "lesson" is to teach her to increase the length of time she can go without you.

Your baby must be feeling terrific as she begins to develop her own little bag of tricks. She discovers she can soothe herself for a short while by sucking on or just looking at her fingers, by puckering up her lips, by opening and closing her eyes, or maybe by gazing at a pattern that's within her range of vision (about one foot).

Sucking

Many crying babies just need something to suck, which is why babies find their fingers. Sucking isn't just for nutrition. It fills a neurological and psychological need as well. Now that we regularly do sonograms we can see baby in the womb, sucking on her thumb. It's part of a natural process of growth and change.

Some babies have a greater need to suck than others. A pacifier is useful for some hardcore suckers. It's a good substitute for her hands, although some parents do object to the look of a "plugged-up" baby.

If you do use pacifiers, buy them by the half dozen. (I like to joke that there is a "Nuk" monster in everyone's home who lives under the crib and steals pacifiers.) Never dip a pacifier in honey and *never, ever* tie it round her neck on a string. It's also a good idea to remove the pacifier from her mouth once she has fallen asleep.

There's a lot of trial and error in figuring out just how to comfort a crying baby. Go through your mental checklist. If she has recently been fed, doesn't want to suck, and her diaper isn't wet, consider that she might just want to be held and cuddled.

Gas

A baby who is being held and is still crying may be gassy. Try jiggling the baby, or rocking her back and forth in her stroller over a doorjamb. (See chapter 5, *Feeding*, for advice) If you hear rumbling or grumbling noises in her belly, put baby in motion— infant seats, swings and slings are helpful.

There's even a device that mimics car motion because, as any mother will tell you, being driven around in a car is almost always a successful way to calm a gassy baby. This particular device was created by a pediatrician who was tired of driving around his own crying baby. He developed a motor that rumbles at 55 miles per hour and can be attached to the bottom of a crib.

Parents have become ingenious at replicating good vibrations.

Parents have become ingenious at replicating good vibrations. Some parents put their babies in an infant seat on top of a running washing machine or dryer. (Of course, you must "stand by" to be sure the seat doesn't jiggle off!) Others keep a vacuum cleaner running. Some babies will calm just as well at the recorded sound of a vacuum cleaner!

Other Soothing Ideas

Parents develop their own ways of calming their baby, often by singing or dancing with her. Some babies are soothed by repetitive sounds, such as ocean waves. I know mothers who turn on tap water to duplicate the rushing sound of bloodflow that the baby listened to while in the uterus. Other parents play relaxation tapes or lullabies, and find themselves nodding off.

If your baby is just moody, try a change of atmosphere. She could be bothered by bright lights, odors, noise or maybe she's just plain bored.

Recognizing Illness

Of course, you must always make sure that your baby is not trying to communicate to you that she's not feeling well. That is why, if at any time your baby's cry sounds significantly different to you than it had previously, you should immediately go in and investigate. Maybe she is warm, indicating that she has a fever and you need to call the doctor. If you cannot console a baby after you've tried all else, then you still need to talk to the doctor.

> If you can't console a baby after you've tried all else, then you still need to talk to the doctor.

I often get calls, "My baby is still crying. She doesn't have a fever. What could it mean?" I run through the checklist of possible solutions and if the mother has tried them all twice, and the baby is still crying, then I ask her to come in to my office. It could be a cry of pain that needs medical attention.

On the other hand, I get calls at 2:00 A.M. The mom says, "My son has been crying for hours. He has no fever, and he only stops crying when he is on my shoulder. Do you think something is wrong?" I am able to reassure her. "It's precisely because he does stop that you know he is all right. Just keep him on your shoulder, and for tonight try to sleep on your feet! Then we all can go back to bed."

Colic

There are babies who cry, and then there are babies who *cry*. A baby who cries inconsolably for long periods is said to be *colicky*. Colic is hard to define because it's not a scientific term. No one really knows what it is, but it is definitely not a disease.

> *No one really knows what colic is, but it's not a disease.*

Colic usually occurs between 2 weeks and 3 months of age and is associated with a cranky baby who is usually crankiest in the evening, although it can be all day. She can cry, wail and shriek for hours at a time. Contrary to some commonly held beliefs, colic isn't caused by bottle-feeding. Breastfed babies can also get colicky. It doesn't seem to be related to feeding at all, because it is not predictable. Parents often change formulas but it does no good. If it were a problem related to feeding, then colic wouldn't happen primarily in the evening. If, however, crankiness occurs only in relation to feeds, then check with your pediatrician. A change of formula just might help.

Even though it's not a digestive problem, I tell mothers to treat colic in much the same way we would gassiness, which means to let the baby move around. Often a mother may need to pace for hours with the baby on her in a front carrier just to achieve peace.

Don't be mad at your colicky baby; it's no one's fault.

Some research indicates that colic occurs in the evening as a result of the body's decreased production of a hormone known as *cortisol*. Most of this hormone is produced in the morning and as the day goes on, less and less is produced and our mood worsens. By the time a newborn has hit 5 o'clock, her cortisol level has dropped to its low point, and she may experience a mood dip.

Because colic also seems to have something to do with the transition from fetal to newborn state, try to recreate the dark, fluid environment of the womb. Take baby into the bath and lay her on your chest. I've also prescribed warm chamomile tea for baby, and it can't hurt mommy either. Do whatever it takes to relax yourself. Turn off the telephone, turn off the television, dim the lights, pull down the shades. You might suggest that people not visit you at that hour.

For more information about colic, visit my Web site at:

http://www.drpaula.com/topics/colic.html

The Effects of Crying

Crying is one of the things babies do best. The problem is the effect that crying babies have on their parents. Some cries are unrelenting. You may be near-crazy with frustration that you can't find a magic wand to wave it away. Cries can set off an earthquake of emotional feelings so that there are aftershocks of tension and despair that erupt over and over.

Anthropologists assure us that crying is, in fact, necessary to keep us on the alert, especially at night when our ancestors really had something to fear out there in the dark.

Some parents begin to fantasize real dangers during these dark "hours from hell." As in all natural things, remind yourself that these hours will pass. Don't ride out the crying storm all by yourself. Enlist help. Maybe your husband can stand behind you and massage your tense shoulders or rub your feet.

It's important not to be mad at your colicky baby or even to think that it is someone's fault. Your bundle of joy has only temporarily become a bundle of noise.

Coming Attractions

If you have been using pacifiers, at about 4 to 6 months old, your baby may start spitting them out. You can make the transition from using to not using pacifiers easier if you don't automatically stick one in her mouth every time she cries. Pick her up and she may forget the pacifier. If your baby continues to need a pacifier after 6 months, which is not harmful, she is now old enough to put the pacifier in her own mouth. Throw a whole bunch into the crib and let her find one for herself. That's a whole lot easier than being beckoned every few minutes to "replug" a crying baby.

At about three months, your baby's cry will have more nuances, and it may be easier to tell the difference between cries. You can more easily comfort your child from a distance. If you can't physically be there, your voice will often be soothing.

Comforting Herself

Most babies begin to develop the ability to comfort themselves, often just by cooing or playing with their fingers. They can hold off a bit on instant gratification. Learning to gain comfort from sucking her own hand, for example, helps your baby blur the distinction between your actually being there to comfort her and your not being there.

You can also help baby develop a transitional object (often called a *lovee*). Let's say you hold a soft cloth or blanket against you while you feed her. Your baby will associate that cloth with being held and she will learn the object is enough to cause comfort. If you put that cloth into her crib, she may rub her face against it and be just fine without you.

8

Grooming

When your precious baby is handed over to you, loving her, even feeding her, seems natural. But you need to learn all the steps to keeping your baby well groomed. A little advice goes a long way.

The irony of the situation is not lost on mothers who ask, "How can such a little person need so much attention?"

Baby's Hygiene

The first days home are governed by the specifics of aftercare.

Umbilical Cord Care

Wipe the baby's cord with alcohol at the base a few times a day and it will soon detach. It is best to wipe the cord using a soft, cotton-tipped applicator soaked in rubbing alcohol so you can apply the alcohol where it's needed, at the very base of the umbilicus where it inserts into the body. If this is not done properly, the cord will get gooey, begin to ooze, possibly get infected and take longer to fall off.

In some societies, the cord is saved for good luck or for medicinal use. We generally just throw it away. Sponge bathe or wash your baby at this time. Don't immerse baby's body in water (and never, ever the baby's head) until the cord has dried and fallen off, which usually occurs at about 10 days.

Bathing

The first thing you should know about bathing is that it's a wonderful, ritualistic thing to do. When an adult is tense, we say,

Bathing is a wonderful time to get close to your baby.

"Go take a warm bath." Bathing your baby, and even bathing *with* your baby, provides more than just an opportunity to clean off the dirt. It's a wonderful time to get close and for your baby to experience the sensation of skin-to-skin contact. It also provides an opportunity for you to see your baby's whole body and observe her in action. From bathtime to bathtime it may appear, for instance, that her fingers are a little longer or that her hair has more curl.

Getting Used to the Bath

Newborns are very sensitive to temperature changes and going from dry air to water can be met with great distress. Bathing can be very difficult at first, so ease baby in gradually. It's a nice idea

How Often to Bathe Baby and When?

How often? In general, you need to bathe your baby infrequently. I'd say it's safe to bathe her every other day and only twice a week in winter. Babies are often overbathed. When they come into my office for their 2-week checkup, they are dry and scaly. The only reasons to wash your baby are to wipe away old diaper ointment, if you are using any; feces; vaginal discharge; sweat and oil from the end of the foreskin and, in summer, from the folds of the neck, groin and armpits.

What time of day? I'm often asked, "When is the best time of day to bathe the baby?" It doesn't really matter. The traditional time for bathing is first thing in the morning, as if your baby were getting ready to go out and play and get dirty. It always surprises parents when I suggest they could bathe baby at night, and use it as a time for both of you to unwind. A colicky baby, who is more likely to be irritable in the late evening, seems to calm better after a warm bath in the evening. Bathing should be a wonderful experience that leaves both of you calmer.

Bathtime can be a wonderful opportunity to include Daddy.
Babies love the skin-to-skin contact.

to start just by trickling the water over her so that she gets used to it little by little. You know how most adults stick their toe in first when they go into the ocean. It's the same for baby, only you are sticking her toe in for her.

Some babies hate baths because it makes them feel out of control of their arms and legs, which often jerk while they are being held suspended over a tub. Try holding your baby more firmly pressed against your body as you trickle water over her and eventually lower her into the bath. Some babies don't like baths no matter what you do!

It's also a nice idea to bathe baby while she's still on your body, and with her skin touching you, maybe on your arm. Try holding the baby in a football style with her feet behind your elbow, again so that the baby doesn't lose contact with your skin. Fathers are particularly adept at bathing baby. They are often equipped with big arms.

The baby bathtub. Use a baby bathtub, preferably one that is not too big. The tub should allow about 3 to 6 inches on each side of baby's body, so she can move her arms and not hit the hard sides and startle herself. Place a baby-body-sized sponge in the bottom of the tub. Remove it after each bath, wring it out and then air dry it. Sponges that are permanently fixed to the bathtub are a bad choice because you can't squeeze them out; mold can grow in them.

Babies need almost no soap or shampoo.

Soap. Most people think you bathe a baby like an adult, which means using a lot of soap. The truth is, babies need almost no soap at all. (They also don't need shampoo, despite the many shampoos marketed for newborns, so just rinse the head with water.) Use a droplet of any mild liquid soap with moisturizer in it. It doesn't have to be specifically designed for a baby.

Remember when you soap your baby, the water you wash her off with is also full of soap, so she could end up with a rash. Lift the baby out of her little tub and dump the soapy water. Find a safe spot to put her down—maybe on a towel on the floor—refill the tub with fresh water, place the baby back in, and rinse her off.

One mother solved the slippery-baby problem by buying two tubs—one for soaping and the other for rinsing. As an alternative, you could take a little shower hose and attach it to the kitchen sink. After you have soaped baby, take the hand shower and rinse her gently. Babies usually love that. (Test the water temperature on your own arm first.)

Never get out of the tub while holding the baby.

Tub toys. In the first 3 months, a baby doesn't need tub toys. The baby needs *you*. Sing, coo to baby, or even take a bath together. Bathing with baby on top of you is a wonderful experience, but some new mothers are still physically uncomfortable and have difficulty climbing in and out of the bathtub with a baby in their arms. I prefer two adults—one in the tub and one to hand the baby to. If you are alone, then put a baby seat outside of the tub and use it to put the baby in while you get in and out. **Never** get out while holding the baby.

If you do decide to take baby into the tub, remember that babies cannot swim or hold their breath, so don't ever let her head submerge. Bathing together is neither unhealthy nor unhygienic for your baby. It's actually quite delightful.

Dry baby thoroughly, especially in the creases—such as the armpits and behind the earlobes—areas that are chronically overlooked.

After the Bath

After the bath, unless the baby's skin is dry and flaky, you don't need to apply oils, lotions or powders.

If your baby tends to be dry, then you might apply an alcohol-free, water-based moisturizer after bathing. Remember, if you spent 9 months submerged in a water environment, you too would get pretty dry skin shortly after emerging! By 3 to 4 weeks, some babies' skin has turned almost lizardlike. Her skin may peel and flake, especially at her wrists and ankles. Apply any water-based lotion a couple of times a day to these areas.

> **Warning**
>
> Don't put a moisturizer on your baby's face and take her out for a walk. That's the equivalent of buttering her up. You are literally frying your baby. Sunburning a baby's skin is very dangerous, particularly because the layers of skin are thinner and the damage can be long lasting.

Avoid powders. I find there's no place in bathing or grooming baby for powder. Talc can be inhaled by the baby and cause serious ailments to lungs, and cornstarch can promote the growth of yeast wherever moisture gets in the creases.

Avoid cotton balls for now. I don't like mothers to use cotton balls for anything to do with cleaning the baby. Cotton can leave wisps behind and make for a clumsy mess, particularly when cleaning up a bowel movement. Use alcohol-free, perfume-free wipes or a soft, wet washcloth instead.

Boys versus Girls

There's not a big difference between washing boy and girl babies, but here are some tips.

- Keep the vagina clean of stool. When you change your daughter's diaper, gently separate the external labia. A white discharge is normal. But if it is tinged with yellow, green or brown then it has stool mixed in with it and needs to be cleaned away. Otherwise the discharge belongs there as protection for the delicate membranes. Leave it alone.

- Boys who are not circumcised should *not* have their foreskins pulled back. If a boy is circumcised, use petroleum jelly (just after circumcision) to prevent his raw penis from rubbing against the surface of his diaper. On a circumcised boy, also make sure that nothing such as dirt, stool or clothing is trapped around the head of the penis. (I recall one time when a clothing thread was accidentally wrapped around the tip. Ouch!)

Head

If baby has a lot of hair, then towel dry the head. This is a wonderful opportunity to give baby a head massage. With your

Don't be afraid of the soft spot.

hand supporting her neck, rub back and forth using a soft terry towel. Babies seem to like this and it increases the circulation to the scalp, which helps get rid of cradle cap. (Cradle cap is actually extra layers of skin that pile up on the head, especially if you have repeatedly used shampoo and didn't quite get all the soap out.)

Don't be afraid of the soft spot, which is actually pretty hard. I have found that some babies only have cradle cap over the soft spot because no one wanted to touch it, not even to clean or dry the area. If there is enough hair, then comb it with a fine baby comb, or a brush.

Eyes

Babies' eyes don't need direct cleaning, except if the baby has blocked tear ducts and mucus gets stuck in the little corner. This is the only time you might use a wet cotton ball. (Ask your doctor to demonstrate this technique for you.) Never use a dry cotton ball because it could irritate or cut the cornea.

Nails

Babies are born with long, thin, irregularly shaped transparent nails. It's difficult to even see they are there. They may go all the way over the finger, like Rip Van Winkle's. The problem is that babies are also born with the reflex to clutch and grab, so they could scratch themselves. Even in the nursery we cuff babies with the sleeves of a nightshirt.

Take extra care when grooming baby's nails.

Don't peel nails. It's tempting to peel the nails. Sometimes they seem to peel by themselves and when you see a nail half off, then you may think you might as well peel it. Don't use this as a routine method. Nails do harden within 2 weeks and can no longer easily be peeled without damaging the part of the nail that is still attached to the finger. Also resist the urge to take your baby's finger in your mouth and nibble off the nail. Infection can spread from your mouth to the baby's skin.

Use baby nail clippers. Always use a miniclipper or baby nail scissors to cut nails. Many people find that baby is resistant and pulls back. Wait to trim his nails until baby is fast asleep. Then cut the nails every 2 to 3 days in the first 3 weeks because they do grow very fast.

Parents occasionally cut the skin when cutting nails. The bleeding is usually easy to control, but if the bleeding doesn't stop within 3 minutes of putting pressure beneath the cut area, then call your doctor. Otherwise, kiss it and just be more careful the next time.

Toenails. Your baby may or may not be born with long toenails. If they get too long, then cut them as well.

More Information about Baby Hygiene

For more information about baby-care products and methods, visit this Web site:

http://www.yourbaby.com/consumer/articles

(Click to SITE MAP AND SEARCH and check ECZEMA/CRADLE CAP.)

Coming Attractions

After about six weeks, your baby is no longer considered a newborn and there will be many changes to mark the occasion. Your baby's skin should no longer be as dry. Nails are harder, more easily clipped and they don't grow as fast. She is less likely to have cradle cap. Between 2 and 3 months of age, she will begin to shed the extra hair on her back and shoulders. In fact, a newborn with a lot of hair may start to go bald.

By 3 months, your baby is stronger and more alert. You can expect your baby not to need her hand held to control her startle reflex when bathing, although you will still need to hold her head. (All of her newborn reflexes, in fact, are starting to fade.) She will lie comfortably in 1/2 inch of water and may like a more vigorous bath, but she still doesn't need a rubber ducky.

Choosing Diapers

After baby is all cleaned up, she needs to be dressed. First she gets diapered. Parents have a lot of choices in diapers now.

Cloth versus Disposable

Both cloth and disposable diapers have advantages and disadvantages. Cloth diapers, which cost far less than disposables, have the advantage of being soft and comfortable and are probably better for irritable babies. Those are infants who cry easily and will invariably cry at the ripping sound that occurs when you pull off the resealable tabs on disposables.

Environmental Considerations

Some families are reverting to cloth diapers because of environmental concerns and the confusion of choosing among all the fashionable and expensive varieties of disposables. It is not clear whether you are actually helping or hurting the environment if you chose cloth and hire a diaper service.

You have to consider the gas it takes for the truck to come to your house and the detergent they use to clean the diapers. The benefits may not outweigh the potential environmental harm some people attach to the use of disposable diapers.

Advantage of cloth. Some babies have a sensitivity to paper and plastic, especially when ammonia, which is in urine, touches the skin. Also cloth can be better in preventing the kind of rashes that result from an allergic reaction to the plastic or paper. You can't know until you try.

Disadvantage of cloth. The disadvantage of cloth is that the urine and stool don't have anywhere to go. They stay exactly where they are—against the skin. In general, most babies have fewer rashes in disposables.

Advantages of disposables. If you use disposables, you have many choices, depending on whim and the shape of your baby. Certain diapers are designed for babies with wide thighs, while others are for skinnier babies. Buy small packs and check out the

These diaper-producing companies offer additional information on their Web sites:

http://www.huggies.com/diaperswipes/diapers/diapers.stm

http://www.pampers.com/products/index_flash.html

http://www.drypers.com/products/diapers.html

Cloth Care

If you use cloth and you don't use a service, you need to wash the diapers very thoroughly. Get a diaper clip, which holds the diaper in the toilet. Let the toilet flush out most of the excrement. Don't let go, or you could wind up with a big plumbing bill!

Throw the diapers in a basin filled with soapy water. Use a baby-soft detergent, but one that won't destroy the flame-retardant property of the diapers. Soak them. Don't use bleach. Using bleach will get the diapers beautifully white, but it leaves behind an ammonia residue that can lead to diaper rash.

Throw the diapers in a washing machine set on hot, which will kill bacteria so the diaper doesn't become a playground for germs. If you have a backyard, it's still lovely to soap up, rinse and throw diapers outdoors on a bush to dry, but not if you use pesticides.

---

shapes. Most disposables fit well enough no matter which you try. It really doesn't matter if you use so-called "boy" or "girl" diapers. That's just a clever marketing device. But look for ones that have resealable tabs. That's a really good perk, particularly when you need to open and close a diaper more than once.

Unless you are Tom Selleck in *Three Men and a Baby*, you will not have trouble diapering the baby. It's totally self-explanatory. If you use cloth, buy Velcro-tabbed plastic diaper covers to hold the diaper on. No more diaper pins.

Time for a Change

Diapers should be changed whenever baby has stool. If your baby has sensitive skin and develops rashes easily—which you will know after the first week—you will have to change her more often, even when she is just wet. An advantage to disposables is that they keep the urine farther from the baby's body.

Ultra-Absorbent Gel

The new ultra-absorbent versions of diapers have a special kind of gel inside that really does help absorb the feces and the urine. The pitfall is that when the gel gets very wet it can come back through the diaper paper and get on baby's skin.

The gel has a tendency to turn a clay color when concentrated urine hits it. It doesn't really look like blood, but sometimes parents think that's just what it is. So I'll get a call, "There's blood in my baby's diaper." I ask if it's an "ultra" diaper, and does it look red or actually more like clay or makeup? I explain what it is and we both breathe a sigh of relief.

Often you can't even tell the diaper is wet until the baby has urinated about four times, because it soaks so deeply into the diaper layers. That's great because the layer that's closest to the skin remains dry.

How to Change a Diaper

Use a spray bottle of warm water to rinse off feces and urine. The baby will enjoy the sensation. Use a soft baby washcloth or a baby wipe for the finishing touches. Some of the newer wipes are alcohol-free and perfume-free. They cost more but are safer for your baby's skin.

Air is the best drying agent.

Air dry your baby's bottom or fan with your hand. Some people have suggested using a blow dryer set on a very low setting, but there is real danger of burning the baby. Keep the diaper off for about 2 to 3 minutes so that air, which is the best drying agent, gets to the area. If your baby has very sensitive skin apply a barrier, such as petroleum jelly, to her bottom. Otherwise use nothing. Again, powder isn't necessary.

Diaper Rash

Most babies experience diaper rash. It is usually marked by general redness, but the rash may be blotchy or spotty. The rash can spread up from the diaper area to the belly button or down onto the thighs and is usually worse in the creases.

Diaper rash is caused by skin contact with urine and feces and is usually not painful to the baby. But it can be ugly to look at. If not treated, the rash can become raw and painful, and even infected. Consult your pediatrician if the rash is bleeding, oozing, blistered or if gets worse after 2 to 3 days of care.

Treating Diaper Rash

- Change diapers frequently and leave baby naked as much as possible.
- Rinse area with water, preferably sprayed on.
- Avoid using wipes.
- Never rub the area.
- Air dry area.
- Liberally coat the diaper with an ointment containing zinc oxide, then pat the diaper onto the skin.
- Apply over-the-counter hydrocortisone cream and antifungal ointment if the rash persists after 48 hours, and consult your pediatrician if the condition has not improved.

For more about diaper rash, visit the drpaula.com Web site:

http://www.drpaula.com/topics/newrashes.html

This is a good Web site also:

http://www.chkd.org/waytogrow/healthy/facts/diaper.htm

Coming Attractions

When your baby approaches 2 months of age, the urine becomes more concentrated and is produced in larger volume. It's the same for stool. As a result, you have to change diapers more often. Most babies who get a diaper rash get it after 2 months.

Clothing

Don't spend a lot of money buying the layette. Often a close relative will offer to buy it for you. If you are doing the purchasing, let me warn you, you do not need the quantities suggested by the salesperson.

Careful about sizes. Even if you aren't paying for the layette, it should still be what you want. Knowing the approximate size of your soon-to-be born baby (and with sonograms you often can) will facilitate shopping. A baby expected to be born weighing more than 6 pounds should have a layette made up mostly of items in the 3- to 6-month size. The average baby is *not* "newborn" layette size.

Although you want to be practical, it's really a lot of fun to shop for baby clothes. In fact, the infant sections in stores are particularly appealing. Baby clothes are designed to act as a magnet to attract you! If you find yourself drawn to a tiny Victorian dress or maybe a miniature tuxedo, smile and go for it.

Choose cotton. Choose *cotton* fabrics. Avoid all synthetics, polyester, acrylic and even wool, which many babies are sensitive to. Yes, baby clothes come in uncomfortable fabrics because they are less expensive. They may also be less flame-retardant. They are not as comfortable as cotton and tend to cause an allergic skin reaction. This is called *contact dermatitis* and is an irritating skin rash.

> I tell new mothers, who are often overheated—even in the winter—as a result of hormone swings, to use their husbands as their temperature gauge and add just 1 more layer to the baby than what dad is wearing. Preemies will need 2 layers.

All your baby really needs are undershirts and comfortable bedclothes, and a few cute outfits for company. Unless you live in a very cool environment, you don't need blanket sleepers, which tend to keep in too much heat. Also remember that for newborns there's really no difference between day and night, so a 2-month-old doesn't need "nighttime" PJs.

Take care not to overdress baby. We tend to overdress babies. Rather than protecting them from the cold, this can cause fever, rash and irritability. Think in terms of several thin layers. Babies don't maintain a steady temperature the way adults do.

Shopping List

- **2 dozen cotton cloth diapers**—for spit-ups and to put under the baby's head in the crib. This is so you don't have to launder the bedding constantly.

- **10 cotton undershirts.** The simplest to put on are those that tie on the side. (Again, don't buy any in newborn size unless baby weighs less than 6 pounds.) Snaps are easy, but they tend to tear off in the wash and leave holes.

- **12 nightgowns**—not the ones with drawstrings on the bottom. If you buy or receive those, then take out the cord because the little drawstring can get tangled in baby's toes, legs and so on. Snap bottoms are okay if it's cold and you like baby's feet to be covered. It's uncomfortable for baby to be either too snug or lost in her clothes. Look for a size approximately 2 months ahead of your baby.

- **6 one-piece stretch suits with snaps, not zippers,** which can catch in baby's skin. (European clothes often have zippers and are sized smaller than those made in North America.) Be sure the snaps go all the way down the legs so that it's easy to change diapers and that the head opening is wide enough to permit your baby's head to slide through without difficulty. (I've seen babies "trapped" in their clothes and squealing to get free.)

- **6 cotton receiving blankets** that are warm, easy to wash and stretch. Don't get the fuzzy flannel kind. They don't wear as well.

- **6 absorbent terry-cloth bibs.** Choose ones with stretchable necks that go over the head easily, but are absorbent enough to catch whatever drips down.

- **1 plain cotton hat.** Your baby's head comprises a great percentage of her body right now and she can lose a lot of heat through her head.

- **Socks or booties are okay, but absolutely *no* shoes.** (The very worst are booties or shoes made with plastic bottoms. They keep the moisture in and the air out. Even a baby can develop athlete's foot.) Your baby does not need shoes until at least 9 or 10 months, when she begins to take her first steps and needs foot protection on the sidewalk.

Coming Attractions

Your baby grows rapidly. Clothes can be as much as 6 months undersized, so don't buy too much adorable stuff in small sizes. People often buy the wrong size, which explains why you will find resales of never-worn baby clothes in newborn sizes.

Your little explorer needs comfortable, loose-fitting clothes.

   Buy for 12 months and up. As baby gets older, she needs more active wear. All clothing should be loose-fitting in order to provide for her new agility. She needs to be able to roll and stretch and move up in the world. Avoid doodads and sew-ons, which can be tugged off and swallowed by your little explorer.

9

Enjoying Your Baby

It may seem like all your baby does is eat, sleep and cry and that most of your time is taken up in maintenance. The truth is there really is a lot of time just to enjoy your baby. The brass ring in the daily parenting merry-go-round is all those hours you spend being with and loving your baby. You not only have a newborn, you also have a brand-new friend—a buddy, a tiny partner in life.

Outings

I often surprise new mothers when I tell them they can take their baby outdoors the first day after they get home. There is absolutely no medical reason not to. As long as the weather is comfortable enough for you, it's comfortable enough for baby. Not only can you take the baby out, you should. It's good for both of you. The change of environment and air is stimulating.

It's been said that when you go out for a long time during the day, baby sleeps better at night. I'm not convinced that's true, but it certainly won't make babies sleep less well at night.

There's also good evidence that changing your baby's environment gives her body the opportunity to regulate her thermostat. When you are in the same climate all the time your immune system isn't as active as when your body is given a little challenge.

Mommy Care

Think of your outings as part of mommy care as well. It is beneficial both for your physical and psychological well-being. To start with, it helps clear your head—literally and figuratively.

In addition, both you and your baby need sunshine, but with caution. (More about that later.) You can't get "rays" sitting indoors. Even on a not-so-sunny day, the sun is still out there. You are also getting exercise, you get to see and be seen and you can show off your new status.

My advice to brand-new mothers is to get out, even if you have to force yourself. Some mothers tell me they are too embarrassed to go out because of their appearance. As one mother put it, "I look at the baby and say, 'This is *so* right.' Then I see *myself* in the mirror and think, 'I look so wrong.'"

It isn't always easy to get yourself "together" enough to be seen in public. (As another mom confessed at a new-mothers group, "It can be 12:30 in the afternoon and I haven't even washed my face yet.")

The argument for not going out is that by the time you do get it together, half the day is gone or it's time to nurse again. The logistics of just leaving the house can be overwhelming. It really helps if you just relax and learn to go with the flow of your baby's schedule.

Don't expect to look exactly the way you did before you had the baby. Plan in advance what outfits you will wear when you go out. You don't want to waste time worrying about clothes—or staring into your closet hoping your pre-pregnancy clothes will magically grow bigger waistlines. If you can afford to, treat yourself to something new. You can even let your fingers do the shopping and buy through mail-order catalogues.

Where to Go, Where Not to Go

Plan and think about what you can do with your baby, or just head out of the house without direction. This is one of the few times in your life when you can sit on a bench or blanket with your baby and do nothing. Of course you *are* doing something—

you are learning how to enjoy your baby. (As one mom mused, "Once Jesse is up, I 'own' her for the day.")

🍂 The park is one of the very best places to go. Not surprisingly, mothers and babies are a common sight there. You will invariably meet other mothers, and you can exchange information or just smiles. Many lasting friendships have blossomed in parks, right alongside the flowers.

🍂 Although many restaurants welcome families, others practically "wish" you away. If you look in and spot crayons on the table or a children's menu in the window, you are in friendly territory. In the first few months, you will find that baby should cooperate by sleeping a lot. The motion of your walking and strolling often makes them sleepy, so it's fairly easy to go out and stop at your local café for a cup of coffee. Again, most restaurants will be accommodating and you will quickly get to know which places put out a tiny welcome mat for babies and which don't. (You probably shouldn't check your infant in the coatroom the way Diane Keaton did in the movie *Baby Boom*.)

🍂 Shopping is usually not the best activity for you and your baby. Many stores won't even let you in with a carriage or a stroller. And there are even some places, such as buses and trains, where you are required to fold the stroller and carry the baby.

🍂 Some movie theaters specifically ban babies and cellular phones because both can go "off" without warning. If you do take your baby to the movies (and no, it won't hurt her to "see" an R-rated one), be considerate enough to walk out if she does start to cry. For quick getaways, sit on the aisle.

🍂 A question I am asked frequently is, "Whom can I expose my baby to?" I advise you to limit the total number of contacts before your baby is 3 months old because her ability to fight off illness is limited. For that reason I would avoid going where there will be large crowds or close quarters. In the excitement of being a new mother, you may wish to take advantage of all the activities you see advertised for families. However, this is not the time for circuses, magic shows, museums or even ball games unless you want to go for your own enjoyment.

Advice from "Perfect" Strangers

As soon as a pregnant woman begins to show, she turns into a public person in every sense of the word. There is almost a community celebration surrounding her. Becoming a parent is another rite of passage.

When you have a new child, it becomes perfectly acceptable for almost anyone to approach and speak to you. I recall the first time my husband and I took our 5-month-old son David out to eat. It was as if the entire restaurant had adopted him, and we weren't eating dinner alone anymore. Practically everyone offered to hold him, even though I was unwilling to let him go.

And we all know that these "adoptive" parents also feel perfectly free to offer advice (which pregnant women are subjected to all the time). When the baby is with you, the advice gets more specific. It may be unsolicited but it is not always unwelcome. Unfortunately, the advice is often conflicting. For each person who admonishes you to zip up your baby because he's cold, another will come along to chide you that he's clearly overdressed.

Should you zip or unzip your baby just to please others? Obviously, no one could, or should, follow all the advice of strangers. Mostly, I recommend you smile and thank the stranger for the suggestion.

There's no reason to get defensive and discount all advice. Try to see most advice for what it usually is: a way for strangers to strike up a friendship, however brief, with you and your child. The actual advice really doesn't matter.

Children are perceived, by and large, as adorable and innocent. The child becomes the channel through which strangers can approach another adult. (Of course, it is never okay for strangers to put their hands on your baby, and you should stop anyone who does.)

Your world will instantly and spontaneously expand when you become a parent. Your child becomes an hub around which many new (and often quite wonderful) relationships are formed.

You will have plenty of opportunities later to take your child to all those magical events.

🌶 We all enjoy sharing our children with others in the family, but whenever possible go to your relatives (instead of having them come to your house), because then you can decide when to leave. In general I would be wary of family birthday parties where there may be lots of toddlers around. Remember, toddlers are particularly "infectious" little people.

🌶 In warm climates and in the summertime, beaches and pools are wonderful for *you*, but you have to be particularly careful with newborns because they burn very easily. Keep your baby in the shade so she gets indirect, not direct, sunlight, especially when the sun is strong.

Use a PABA-free sunscreen, specifically designed for babies, and apply generously to any baby parts that are uncovered. But baby should not be spending enough time in the sun to get a tan at this age, let alone a sunburn. If there is a chance of considerable sunshine, make sure the baby is wearing a cotton cover-up, or consider not going out at all.

🌶 Many public pools don't allow babies who are still in diapers to go into the water. Keep in mind that temperature regulation in newborns is not well developed. Even most YMCA's don't offer baby swimming classes until after 6 months because of the instability of baby's temperature. (Baby's temperature normally ranges from 97F/36.1C to 100F/37.7C)

Heat flows from a hotter source to a cooler source. When you put your baby into cool pool water, she can't regulate her temperature and she will lose her own heat to the pool. It's one thing to dribble a little water on her or run her toes through the ocean edge, but I would not take a newborn into the water.

If you *do* take baby into a pool, the water should be sufficiently chlorinated so that bacteria won't grow. Always rinse off your baby with fresh warm water because chlorine dries out the skin.

Going Out

What to Take

I recommend that you keep a bag packed and ready to go for outings with baby. It's the equivalent of a doctor's little black bag. If you are bottle-feeding and you use a powdered formula, measure some into a bottle so that all you have to do is add water from a water fountain or any restaurant. Even simpler: Buy a couple of nursette-size, ready-to-feed bottles. They last for months. (Check the expiration date.) Make sure you include

- plenty of diapers
- wipes or a wet washcloth in a zip-style plastic bag
- a spit-up cloth
- a change of clothes for baby
- a plastic bag or two for wet clothes

Replenish this bag whenever you come home.

Many of the new bags take the place of a pocketbook and come with printed compartments. You can't lose things, like your keys, because you simply attach them to the "KEYS" section. Tuck in some money, a small spray perfume or lipstick, if that's what makes you feel good.

One mom confessed that whenever she passes herself in a store window and looks "bedraggled," she reaches for her brightest red lipstick. I always carried a pair of earrings. If I went into a store or restaurant and felt I wanted to look a little special, I slipped them on. I suddenly felt different—more dressed up.

As you venture out more often, you will know exactly what you need to put into that bag. For example, you might include baby sunscreen, a bottle of water and a magazine. You might want to have mosquito netting that fits over the stroller in case of "attack."

Carrying Your Baby

There are a variety of ways, from carriages to Snugli front carriers, slings and strollers, to take baby out. It's a matter of personal choice, but your baby's safety should always be first. Keep in mind, for example, that people can fall over a stroller before they even know it's there. To an outsider, your stroller can look like there is a hole in the crowd. I've heard mothers screaming, "Can't you see there is a baby down there?" If you really need to go to crowded events, like baseball games, baby belongs in a carrier on your body.

If you use a carriage, put mosquito netting over it. It's not just to keep mosquitoes out, but real-life "pests" as well. (There will always be strangers who insist on peeking in and even touching your baby.)

A word about carriages: Some beautiful new European ones are made with "windows." The baby can look out to see the world and you can see baby through the sides. Babies are usually in the carriage for just a short time as a newborn, and by the time they can sit up and appreciate the passing landscape, they are too big for the carriage.

You can carry baby around in a portable bassinet. Even lighter-weight car seats, which are easily removable or have a snap-out section, can be used for walking around as well as for riding in the car. If your baby is sleeping, you can just pick her up and bring her into the restaurant or wherever you are going.

It's very popular to "wear" your baby. Women have been wearing their babies since they began having them. There are some terrific carriers for newborns modeled on those of other cultures. Even before we had the wheel, we had the sling. Women wore their babies tied very snugly to their backs, with the baby's head held steady with a big shawl. Nowadays, there are wonderful slings that go across one shoulder and look like little hammocks. They can also be worn by fathers.

In one version, called *Sarah's Ride™*, the seat goes on your hip. It was originally designed for 6-month-olds who could sit up, because it didn't provide back support, but now it's a whole miniature hammock. It's particularly good for people with back problems because the weight is on the hip rather than the

After nine long months, Daddy can enjoy taking a turn at carrying the baby. As the baby's head control improves, side carrying becomes more comfortable.

For variety, let your baby look outward at her new world. This position also lets you show her off a bit.

shoulders. You and the baby's father should try on various carriers and see what feels right.

🌶 Snuglies, or other front carriers, come in different shapes and sizes. Look for convertible styles that adapt to different seasons. Some Snuglies are designed to let baby's arms and legs hang out. In addition to the traditional position of facing in, one newer Snugli allows for the baby to face out.

I have a mom who always arrives with her infant on her chest facing outward. I say, "Hi, it's mommy and 'Velcro' baby!" It looks like Jennifer is snapped onto her chest. Mommy waves, and Jennifer smiles at me. This type of carrier is particularly good for the 2- to 3-month-old baby, who can now look around and enjoys seeing more than just mommy's blouse.

Coming Attractions

One reason I recommend you go out often now when your baby is a newborn is that once she is older, she will be aching to get out of the stroller. In general, she will not be as easy to tote around. You have about a 6-month window, max, so keep it open! When you take a 6-month-old baby out to a restaurant, for example, you will have to move just about everything on the table out of range. You may spend as much time watching and worrying as eating. (Sassy Seats®, which hook up under the table, are not good until the child is fully sitting up at about six months.)

A newborn is easier to bring along, so don't miss your chances!

By 3 months, your baby will have fairly good head control, so that you can put her in an apparatus that is more liberating. After 3 months, you can even consider putting her in a backpack.

Car seats are still essential! She still needs to be in a harness car seat when she rides in a car, but it can face forward. If you are driving alone and can't put the baby in the seat next to you, because of risk of injury from air bag inflation, you can still view the baby by looking in the rearview mirror.

Your infant belongs in the center of the backseat secured in an approved and properly installed infant car seat. Do not make creative adaptations when installing the seat or you risk injury to your precious child.

Baby more alert. A 3-month-old is more alert. She can sit in a propped-up position and grab at toys. She will be awake for longer periods and can appreciate and swat at a little colorful bar across her stroller. She is still not ready for a 3-ring circus but now a stroll down the street is for more than just a breath of air. She can't wave, but people will wave at her. So continue to go to the park, and take her on picnics. The same rules apply to the beach. Continue to keep her out of the sun—her skin is still extremely sensitive.

Your baby is now ready to face more of the world.

> For more information about infant car seats and child safety in automobiles, click on these Web sites:
>
> **http://www.aap.org/family/famshop.htm**
>
> **http://www.aap.org/family/01352.htm**
>
> **http://nhtsa.dot.gov/people/injury/childps**

Immunities improve. Your baby's immune system is stronger at 3 months, so she can go celebrate at birthday parties and all the other places I previously warned you against. She can even be exposed to multiple children without the same degree of paranoia you need for a child under 2 months. You can practically pass the baby around the table like a salt or pepper shaker!

Enjoying Baby Indoors

When you and your baby are staying in and she is awake, you can really put her anywhere you like. My favorite place is on a blanket on the floor. Up to 3 months, babies can't go anywhere without you. Although playpens have gotten a bad name lately, they are a fine, safe place as long as you don't use them as a jail.

(If you leave a crying baby in a playpen she really will feel like a little prisoner.)

You can also use an infant carrier or car seat inside the house. This double duty is especially helpful for those parents with limited living space. Baby paraphernalia does seem to take over, almost like creeping vines.

> A playpen is just right, even for a newborn, as long as it's safety approved. That means there are no bars for her to get trapped in, and no internal hinges that could collapse. In fact, the earlier you start putting a baby into a playpen, the less difficulty you will have with the occasional use of one later on.

Jolly jumpers are good at about 3 months, but walkers, *never*, especially if you have stairs. They may provide a fun time for your baby while she is in it, but it is not worth the potential risk. Walkers have been known to take babies places where no baby should be able to go!

Fathers and Play

A word about fathers: It's been well observed that fathers play differently with babies than mothers do. They are often more vigorous. This doesn't mean that they hurt the baby, just that they give the baby a more rigorous workout.

If your mate wants to spin around with the baby in the air, don't discourage him. Even if it looks scary to you, it's more important that it isn't scary to the baby. (It's a good time to snap pictures of him smiling with his father.) Fathers have instincts, too—they want to protect their precious baby as much as you do. They just do it differently.

Baby Needs Touch

Babies really like to have their bodies touched and caressed. They are sensual and arousable. Newborn baby boys occasionally get erections. We now know that touching babies is basic to their very survival. In one recent study, premature babies who were massaged were ready to go home earlier than those who weren't.

Holding Baby

You should be spending a lot of time being physically close to your newborn. Babies should come with "please touch" signs. You can pick them up and hold them in a variety of positions that are enjoyable and alleviate your occasional boredom.

There are at least four holds you can use when baby doesn't want to be put down.

1. The Airplane Hold. One hand is under the belly, legs sprawled apart over the crook of the arm, with your hand holding her face. To the initial horror of a mother in my new-mother's group, I took her baby and "flew" him up and down. He loved it. This hold usually calms a crying baby almost immediately.

2. Variation on the Airplane. Face baby toward you, holding his head in your palm with his legs straddling the bend at the elbow. He is upright and you are holding his hand with him facing you. Then you can raise him up and down.

3. The Swing. Sit on the edge of a chair with your legs apart, and hold the newborn under his armpits with your thumbs at the back of his neck. Swing him gently forward and back.

4. The Traditional "Ride." Baby is sitting up on your shoulders, wrapped over your head with your hands behind him, maybe looking in a mirror.

These holds are also good for *you*. If you can't get out, you can still exercise—weight lift—with your baby as the weight.

You can also lie on your back and hold your baby under his armpits. His head may flop a little forward, but his neck will not break. (You really don't have to do that much head-holding. The head does kind of loll over, and it *looks* fragile, but you will notice that he is not crying.) Gently do "bench presses" by lifting your baby up and down.

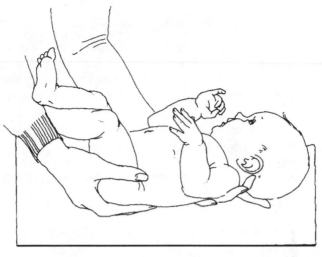

Enjoy giving your baby a "ride" and always remember to support the head and neck.

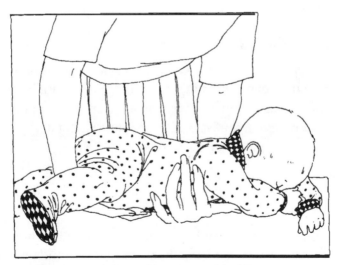

Babies enjoy being held and moved in different positions. This position may also help relieve gas or colic.

> ### Kisses, Kisses, and More Kisses
>
> It should go without saying that the more kisses you give the baby—at any and all times—the better. You may leave no spot unkissed. I've had mothers come in and say, "I feel it's not normal to kiss the baby below the belly button." If you feel uncomfortable, then don't do it. But if you *are* comfortable, then don't let anybody else tell you it's not normal, for example, to kiss a baby's behind.

Indoor time is also a good time to go skin-to-skin with your baby. In simpler societies, people don't wear a lot of clothes to begin with, and babies spend a lot of time on their parent's back or front. The sense of comfort and safety that these children have has been well observed. Being skin-to-skin adds to the development of trust and intimacy and is a healthy, pleasurable bonding behavior.

Baby Massage

A wonderful indoor activity is to give your baby a massage. If you can, set aside time every morning or evening. There are basically two kinds of massages: One is soothing and best done before bath-, nap- or bedtime; the other is more stimulating and appreciated after a nap when baby is more alert.

- You don't need to use lotion unless her skin is very dry and then you can combine moisturizing with massaging.

- Put your baby down on her back and start with light strokes. Be aware that some babies don't respond well to a feather-light touch—it's almost what tickling would be for an adult. Maintain eye contact with her and speak softly or coo to her. Measure the response you get and respond in kind.

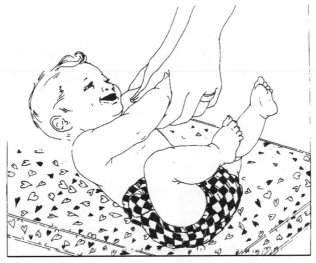

By 3 months, your baby's head control is well developed.

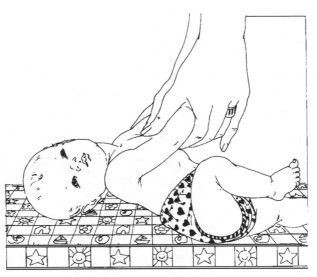

Play with your baby by gently lifting her shoulders, but let her head rest on the surface until she is older and her neck can support her head.

❧ Don't be afraid of the soft spot on her head. In fact, many babies will calm down when the top of the head is stroked.

❧ Babies are flexible. You can take her toe and touch the top of her head with it. But do it gently, in a smooth and symmetric way. First one side, then the other, or both at the same time, move baby's legs up and down or push the knees to one side. Think of your baby as an infinitely more flexible version of yourself. You are exercising and massaging at the same time.

Bathtub Fun

I also encourage playing in the bathtub with your newborn after the cord has dried. In fact, one of the best activities on a dreary rainy day is to get into the bathtub with your baby. Remember, if there's no other adult around, put a baby seat outside the tub, lean over and put the baby in the seat and then get out. (While you are in the bath, you could use a hand shower to gently spray water over the baby.)

Toys and Nurseries

You want to ensure that your baby's transition from the womb to the world is a peaceful one, so include in the transition the sounds, sights and smells of gentle life.

Make sure that when baby opens her eyes, they aren't staring at a plain, white world. Use lots of bright, contrasting colors. Interestingly, it's believed that black-and-white patterns are easiest for babies to look at because they provide the most contrast. It's not so much that babies like black per se, but black is as different from white as you can get. (You might want to throw a nice, soft penguin or striped zebra toy into baby's crib.) If you buy a mobile, make sure it faces downward so your baby can see it.

> I'm often asked, "What does my newborn need to play with?" The answer is *you*. You are the greatest light-and-sound show in the world. Newborns need to be stimulated by living beings.

Choose mobiles and stuffed animals that make soothing noises. Look for specially designed teddy bears that duplicate uterine sounds. These have been likened to an audible "pacifier." Lullabies are traditionally sung because they have a repetitive lilt. Your newborn is not ready yet for recording star Raffi—the 'N Sync of the toddler set.

The most fun toy you can give your baby is a mirror.

The newborn, up to about two months, does enjoy reflective objects that let her see herself. The most fun toy you can give your baby is a mirror. I've seen cribs made with mirrors on the side. Obviously they are not made of glass but from a synthetic reflecting material.

What's appropriate now are soft, plush toys that have no small parts that can fall off and be swallowed. Again, choose bright or contrasting colors and materials that reflect in some way. There are even stuffed animals that have reflective mirrors on them.

Coming Attractions

At first your baby's reactions are to you. *You* are the toy. Before 3 months or so, if you throw a rattle into the crib, she may simply roll into it and wake up. She certainly can't hold it in her hand and shake it. If you like, you can hold the rattle over the baby and shake it for her.

At 2 months, toys can gradually change into action/reaction toys. She touches it and something happens: A light comes on or a bell rings or an object pops up. To be satisfying for baby, this motion should be very easy for baby to do.

At the very beginning, the child will hit the toy by accident and then learn, "When I touch that shape, a bell rings." Eventually the playing will progress from random touching to a deliberate action. These toys are not only fun but also they make babies feel powerful. They give babies a way of interacting with the world. It's similar to when your baby first cries and learns that you respond. Now your baby adds another valuable insight.

At 3 months, some parents begin to enroll their babies in gym programs. I'm a firm believer that they aren't necessary. You can continue to be your child's own "Nautilus machine" by lifting and working out with her. As babies get older they usually like to be massaged more. Your strokes can get stronger and can last for a longer period of time.

10

Your Baby's Health— Wellness and Illness

New mothers often tell me that they worry about being responsible for another person's life. They are concerned that they will not always be able to tell if something is wrong. I remind them: You are not alone in taking care of this baby. You should be in a partnership with your pediatrician.

In addition to the standard series of visits, you are never more than a phone call away from the doctor. If, at any time, there is something about the baby that bothers you or makes you uncomfortable, call!

Pediatrician Visits

Your regularly scheduled visits with the doctor, which are usually at 2 weeks of age and then at 1-month intervals for the first 6 months, are wonderful opportunities to ask your questions and reassure yourself that all is well.

> The American Academy of Pediatrics provides good suggestions for choosing the right pediatrician for your baby at this Web site:
>
> **http://www.aap.org/family/youandpd.htm**

> ### The Case of the Amazing Shrinking Baby
>
> I've had mothers in my office wonder, "How did my baby shrink?" She didn't. Most babies are recorded at birth as being 20 inches. That's because it's difficult to measure accurately and the nurse often can only approximate the height. But you may go to your doctor's office for the first visit and think your baby has somehow shrunk!

The 2-Week Visit

The main focus of this visit is to check baby's progress and make sure she has regained her birth weight. Assuming she has, then the next visit will be 1 month later. At the 2-week visit, and at each subsequent visit, you'll be told your baby's length and head measurement. She will have grown about 1/2 an inch in length and about 1/2 centimeter in head circumference.

A thorough examination. You will be asked to completely undress the baby, so dress her in clothes that are easy to remove. The entire visit should be full of information as the doctor examines your baby's body from top to bottom. You and the pediatrician can really observe the baby together.

- Your doctor will explain, for example, that the eye color is changing, and the eyes are not yet in full focus.
- Did the umbilical cord fall off completely or does it still need to be wiped with alcohol?
- Did the belly button heal well or does it need a little treatment?
- Is the circumcision healed?
- Are there rashes in her creases and folds or maybe a dryness all over the skin?
- Does the baby's scalp need some attention to get rid of cradle cap?

Feeding discussion. The doctor will discuss feeding patterns and reassure you, or give additional advice on how feeding should proceed. You are most likely to hear that whatever you are doing you should keep on doing. If you bottle-feed and there's a need to change formula or switch to one with iron, the doctor will tell you.

A common concern parents have is whether or not the baby is getting enough milk (particularly if you are breastfeeding). An easy way to tell if your baby is taking in enough is to check if she is producing urine and stool. (Because of the high absorption of disposable diapers, you can't always tell if your baby has urinated. Put a tissue into the diaper and check later to see if it is wet.) The acid test, of course, is weight gain, but I strongly discourage using your bathroom scale. It's not accurate enough for "gram" differences, and you'll be getting an exact measure at this and subsequent doctor visits.

Lessons in Calming and Communicating with Baby

You may observe that the doctor knows how to calm your baby in a way that you might want to duplicate.

For instance, when the doctor puts the special viewer or *otoscope* in your baby's ears or the tongue depressor in her mouth, you may see that the doctor lets the baby wrap her fingers around his. The doctor may even put his finger, padside up, into the baby's mouth for her to suck on so he can look into your baby's eyes with the opthalmoscope. This is because a 2-week-old baby will reflexively open her eyes while she is sucking. It's difficult, unpleasant and unnecessary to pry a baby's eyes open to examine them, but as soon as sucking starts, the exam is easily accomplished.

You may also notice that when your baby cries the doctor may "cry" right back—in a slightly softer tone. Babies will sometimes stop crying to listen and will then respond in a slightly different tone. Your baby and doctor are communicating. You can try the same thing later.

The doctor also knows that you can often stop a baby from crying just by getting very close to her. If you are within 6 to 12 inches of a baby, so she can see you clearly, she will enjoy looking at your face.

Vaccination Schedule – First Year

Month	1	2	4	6	10	12
DaPT IPV		✓	✓	✓		
Hep B*	✓	✓			✓	
HIB		✓	✓	✓		
MMR**/varicella						✓
TB Test					✓	

*May be first given in the hospital nursery. Second dose would occur at 1-month visit. Third dose may be given anytime from 6 to 18 months after the first dose.
**May be given between 12 to 15 months, and may be combined with the chickenpox vaccine.

DaPT–*Diphtheria, acellular pertussis + tetanus vaccines*
IPV–*Injected polio vaccine*
Hep B–*Hepatitis B vaccine*
HIB–*Hemophilus Influenza type B vaccine (sometimes referred to as the "meningitis vaccine")*
MMR–*Measles, mumps, rubella vaccine*

The Second Visit

Whereas at the first visit your baby may have appeared to be mostly passive, at this visit she is beginning to flower. At 6 weeks of age, she isn't quite a newborn. You have a whole different baby. The skin is not so flaky and rashes and acne have mostly disappeared.

Another thorough examination. At every visit, the doctor will check the baby's entire body. Eyes, ears, nose, mouth, neck, chest, heart, lungs, abdomen, hips, genitals, extremities—he will visually inspect and examine all.

Baby's patterns are discernable. At 6 weeks, you are able to discern baby's habits and patterns, such as how long she sleeps and eats, when in the day she is most likely to cry. Parents often ask about baby's feedings. Maybe she appears gassy or fitful after feeding. This frequently begins after the first 2 to 3 weeks of life, so naturally it comes up at this visit. "How do I get my baby to sleep through the night?" is a popular question. It's the doctor's job to give you the bad news: Most babies *don't* sleep through the night at this point.

Developmental progress is noted. At this visit you will undoubtedly want to know what your baby can do, understand and see. The doctor will check your baby for developmental achievements. She should be making eye contact, smiling, and maybe making some rudimentary cooing sounds. You and your baby may have forged deeper bonds because you can communicate more easily. Some babies now respond more readily to sound.

Some babies now respond more readily to sound.

Although they are less jittery (their startle reflex is fading), they are truly more alert. They are no longer just victims of their own delicate nervous system. They are, in fact, startled more easily by externals such as the sound of a fire engine or vacuum cleaner. They may even wake up if you talk loudly.

The 2- to 3-Month Visit

Developmental progress is again noted. At this visit, the doctor will concentrate on developmental signs. The 2- to 3-month-old baby is significantly different in terms of motor skills than a newborn. She should establish eye contact deliberately. She should smile, and not just at anyone, but have a special smile just for you.

She should be able to reach for and swat at things. Her grasp will be less reflexive and more deliberate. If you hold out a rattle, she might reach with her hand and get it. Some babies will even begin to roll over, alerting you to babyproof around the changing table. You can also expect her to look better. Infantile rashes should be gone and her cradle cap all clear.

Vaccinations. This visit ends with vaccines against DaPT and polio (see box on page 166). Sometimes 3 vaccines will be injected at this visit, the third being the HIB shot. The doctor usually gives these shots in the outer thigh and then hands baby back to you quickly. It often happens so fast you won't see the shot, but you will know it has been administered when your baby wails. For more about vaccinations, refer to the chart on page 164.

DPT

DPT stands for *Diptheria* / *Pertussis* / *Tetanus* and is a vaccine that has a reputation for side effects. Recently an acellular version, DaPT, has eliminated side effects almost entirely.

The pertussis portion prevents the disease commonly known as *whooping cough*. The most common side effects, if any, are very minor—low-grade fever, irritability and swelling or tenderness at the site of injection, usually at Tetanus response.

Note: Your doctor should give you detailed instructions on aftercare. If your child appears irritable, check the leg. If it is swollen or red, apply a cool compress, and give a dose of fever-reducing medicine. The dose, determined by baby's weight, will be recommended by your doctor. Some doctors suggest you give a dose of an acetaminophen before you come in for the visit. Others give it in the office and still others shortly after.

It is very rare to have a serious reaction, and you cannot miss it. The doctor will tell you the warning signs. I advise all parents: Don't worry that something bad might happen and you won't know it. You would and usually it won't.

Let me make this very clear: This vaccine is required by law and is not dangerous. On the contrary, DPT has saved an overwhelming number of lives. The mortality statistics since the introduction of the vaccine are amazing. As far as I'm concerned, there is no controversy about its use. However, I have seen perfectly normal babies die because they were *not* immunized.

(There are, however, a few legitimate reasons not to be immunized with specific agents. If your child has a progressive neurological condition or if a close relative had a serious reaction to the pertussis vaccine, you must discuss this with your pediatrician at the very first visit.)

For updates about children's vaccinations, please visit my Web site at this address:

http://www.drpaula.com/topics/vacupdate99.html

The Sick Baby

You really become a parent at your child's first illness. Sometimes new moms will confide to me that they feel a little like they are playing house, dressing and feeding a doll. But the very first time you sense there could be something wrong with your baby, you are pushed over the fantasy threshold and right into the reality of being a parent. As one woman put it, "I felt like I was play acting, until Jesse got sick. Then I had to console him, and it connected that I was really a mother."

You really become a parent at your child's first illness.

You may even panic and feel like a hand has reached in and clutched your heart. It can also be very frustrating. You say to your crying baby, who looks as if she might be in pain, "Just tell mommy where it hurts" and, of course, the baby can't!

Fever

If your baby feels warmer than usual, take her temperature with a rectal thermometer. Don't decide whether your baby has a fever by feeling baby's head or fingers. Remember that her extremities and head are noticeably different in temperature from the actual "core" temperature. Her hands and feet should usually be cool. If, however, baby's hands and fingers are hot and you haven't overdressed the baby, then you may want to take her temperature to be sure.

When Your Baby Is "Not Quite Right"

There are several indicators that doctors use to determine if a baby is ill. If your baby feels warm, is irritable, can't be calmed or is sleeping excessively, she may be coming down with something. It's time to call your pediatrician. Poor appetite can also be a "lone" signal of illness. Anytime you think your baby is sick, call the doctor to discuss it.

When and How to Take Your Baby's Temperature

Do not take your baby's temperature unless you suspect she is sick. When you do, take it rectally, with the thermometer about 1/2 inch into the rectum for at least 1½ minutes. The "fever strip" and other surface ways to take your child's temperature are absolutely useless in babies. Worse, they often give misleading information. The thermometer that reads the temperature via the ear opening is not yet suitably sized for newborns. For now, use the old-fashioned glass or quicker digital thermometers.

> Remember, your baby's behavior is always the best indication of how well or sick she is.

Before you take your baby's temperature, take off her clothes and let her lie uncovered at least 3 to 5 minutes. And, no, baby won't get a chill while she is undressed. The temperature outside the baby doesn't influence wellness or illness. If you are taking her temperature, it's because you think she may already be sick and you need accurate information.

Note: Babies under 2 weeks have very poor temperature regulation. You can inadvertently overdress them and "make a fever." You can also have a sick baby who doesn't register any fever. So again, pay attention to her temperament.

Remember, your baby's behavior is always the best indication of how well or sick she is. Never discount an irritable baby just because she has no fever. Call and discuss this with the baby's doctor.

Very Important!

Call the doctor if your newborn has a temperature over 100F/37.7C, even if she seems fine. *Any baby under 2 months with a temperature over 101F/38.3C must be seen IMMEDIATELY.* If your doctor is not available, go to the emergency room of the nearest hospital. (Never give any medicine to your newborn without your doctor's specific instructions—not even Tylenol.)

Common Illnesses

The common cold. Many times parents will call reporting what looks and sounds like nasal congestion. Often it's not a cold but just the natural collection of mucus and secretions that all babies make. I get other calls indicating there is something different about the coughing and sneezing: "I know you told me that some coughing and sneezing is normal [in order to clear the airway], but she's coughing and sneezing more frequently and it sounds a little like her chest is rattling. When she sneezes, some yellow stuff is coming out of her nose." Those symptoms alert me—in the absence of irritability or fever—to give some simple advice.

Your baby does not have immunities to viruses you haven't had yet.

The common cold is just that—*common*. It's less likely in the first 2 months because baby still has immunities from you. However, she does not have immunities to viruses you haven't had yet or that someone else is bringing into the house. If there is an older sibling around, it's quite possible she had a cold and passed it to her little sister. (In fact, if you have an older child, your newborn may well be sicker more often and earlier than your first child ever was.) Fall and winter babies also get more colds than spring and summer babies, and they get them at younger ages.

Rashes. If a baby has a rash that persists or looks raw, blistered, pus-filled or bloody, call the doctor immediately. A faint rash often appears in children who are ill. (Diaper rash is not an illness. See chapter 8, *Grooming.*) Describe the rash to your pediatrician as best you can.

Thrush. Thrush is a common yeast infection in the mouth. If baby's mouth has a white coating that resembles glue or milk that hasn't been swallowed hours after drinking and it doesn't easily wipe away, it's probably thrush. It's usually on the tongue and on the inside of the lips and cheeks (the mucous membranes of the oral cavity). The yeast, candida, doesn't cause a fever, but it can lead to significant discomfort while baby is sucking. She won't eat as well as usual. Any time baby isn't eating well,

"Curing" the Common Cold

- Your baby may respond to simple home remedies, such as running a cool-mist humidifier (make sure you clean it daily). The humidity provides thinning action on the thick mucus in the airways. It is easier for thin mucus to run out of the nose or even down the back of the throat and into the stomach where it is harmless—as opposed to into the lungs, where it *isn't* harmless. It mostly provides some relief so that baby can breathe easier and suck more comfortably.

  Never use a hot vaporizer. They are dangerous. You can get burned and the hot water tends to encourage fungus and bacterial growth.

- You can also "steam" baby. Go into the bathroom, close the door and turn on the shower to the hottest setting until the bathroom is much like a steam room. Sit in the bathroom with baby in your arms or on your shoulder. In this case, the hot steam works better than cool steam to thin the mucus.

  Some parents worry that the baby will be all wet when she comes out. "Won't she catch cold?" No. She already has a cold. You don't get sick by being wet, and certainly you can dry her off before you leave the bathroom. Also, she doesn't have to be naked while in the steam.

- You are trying to help baby clear her airways. You can't teach a newborn how to clear her throat or blow her nose, but your doctor may recommend you put some saline drops in her nose. That's a good idea. Others may suggest you elevate the head of the crib. That usually doesn't work. Most babies will just slide down to the bottom of the crib.

- Some parents try to suction out the mucus with a "bulb syringe" like the one used in the hospital at the birth. I find that very little is accomplished and most babies hate it!

first check to see what is going on in her mouth. Call the doctor, who will probably prescribe an antifungal medicine that is given by mouth. If you also have an itchy vaginal discharge or if your nipples itch, you may need your own prescription or you may be advised to take some of the medicine prescribed for the baby and put it on your nipples.

Chickenpox. Yes, newborns can get chickenpox. You can't miss it, because it causes blisters with fluid inside. If your baby has been exposed to chickenpox and is under 1 week of age, call the doctor immediately. An injection can be given to newborns who have been exposed to chickenpox. There is also an antiviral treatment called *Acyclovir* that subdues the infection. But it must be taken very early in the illness. Newborns are known to either get an extremely severe or very mild version.

To comfort a baby with chickenpox, use cool baths, a calamine-type lotion, and Tylenol, if your doctor recommends it. Most doctors are recommending the chickenpox vaccine at 12 to 15 months. There is still some question about the length of immunity the vaccine will give, so be prepared to need a booster sometime in the future.

Allergic reactions. It's rare for a newborn to have allergies to foods because you are only giving them one food: milk. However, some babies become allergic to it in time. But if you've just changed formulas, you could see a reaction. (Sometimes a formula goes on sale and moms assume it's okay to switch. It's not.) You could also see an allergic reaction in the baby if you've taken a drug, such as a cold tablet, and then nursed.

Newborns rarely have allergies to food.

An allergic reaction is distinctive looking. It's not pinpoint or pimplelike. It looks like a "relief map" on baby's skin. The rash—which is raised, warm and itchy— changes before your eyes in location and size. A newborn can't scratch efficiently and he or she may be writhing with irritability. That's worth an immediate call and visit to the doctor, who may prescribe an antihistamine even before you come in.

Vomiting and diarrhea. Most babies spit up. But parents will occasionally call and say, "It looks like gallons of liquid." (Of course it's not gallons.) Sometimes it's described as *projectile*

More Information about Common Childhood Illnesses

Please check the drpaula.com Web site for additional information about these common childhood illnesses, at the following addresses:

Common cold:
http://www.drpaula.com/topics/cold.html

Chickenpox:
http://www.drpaula.com/topics/chickpox.html

Allergic reactions:
http://www.drpaula.com/topics/allergiesnasthma.html

Diarrhea:
http://www.drpaula.com/topics/diarrhea.html

Vomiting:
http://www.drpaula.com/topics/vomit.html

or *shooting across the room*. It's a larger quantity and has more force behind it. You may want to wait after the first vomit before you call the doctor. It could have just been the result of the position the baby was fed in. Maybe a big gas bubble got caught under some milk and forced its way up.

If baby vomits again, it's definitely time to call. It may mean the baby has an infection that is causing gastric upset or it could represent a "mechanical" problem—milk is unable to pass through into the lower intestines. The doctor will tell you more after examining the baby.

It can sometimes be hard to tell if your baby has diarrhea. Breastfed babies have frequent, loose, watery stools. If stools have gotten thinner but are no more frequent, a little stomach upset may be the cause. You can help baby by offering her some water, in addition to breast milk or formula, to compensate a little for her fluid loss. Vomiting in conjunction with loose stools warrants an immediate call to the doctor. (If at any time stool has blood in it, that's also an immediate call, although usually the condition is not serious. On occasion newborns may have a few tiny specks of blood in their stool as they adjust to formula or if stools are hard.)

Your Medicine Cabinet

Don't wait for the first illness to take a trip to the drugstore. You'll need to keep on hand:

- Saline nose drops
- A thermometer
- A fever reducer, such as Tylenol for Infants
- Syrup of ipecac, which is used to induce vomiting
- A lotion to soothe itches and sunburn
- A baby teething gel
- A nonalcohol, nonperfume lotion for dry skin
- Alcohol
- Cotton balls and cotton tip applicators
- Petroleum jelly or lubricant
- Diaper cream
- Nail clippers or scissors
- Topical antibiotic ointment
- Rehydration solution, such as Pedialyte®
- Measuring dropper

Most medicines designed for babies come with droppers. Be sure to rinse these with water after each use. Never use a kitchen spoon to measure amounts.

Also, visit the drpaula.com Web site for more information about these handy products:

http://www.drpaula.com/medcab/

And What If . . . ?

In spite of loving and watching over your baby, bad things can still happen.

➤ You could drop the baby or she could just bang her head by accident. Calm yourself enough to notice what your baby's first reaction is: Did she cry, or did she look stunned and then cry, or did she stop breathing and then start to breathe again when you picked her up? Did she change color? If so, what color: red or blue? If your baby cries immediately on impact, that's a very good sign. If not, particularly if the baby passes out (or loses consciousness, even momentarily), take the baby right to the emergency room.

🦅 As a result of an accident, your baby could be bleeding. Sometimes you just turn sideways in a doorway and the baby "catches" her head. Don't be surprised if there is a lot of blood—especially if the injury involves the scalp. (There may also be a lot of blood when the baby cuts the "frenulum"—the little piece of skin that holds the lips on to the gums and the little piece of skin that holds the tongue down.)

When accidents happen, try to stay calm so you can help your baby.

Immediately apply pressure to the area that is bleeding, and *don't let go* for at least 10 minutes. (Resist the temptation to "peek" at it. If it was bleeding badly and getting near to the point of clotting and you let go, it may start to bleed again.) Don't be afraid to press hard. I would rather you press too hard than not hard enough. If the bleeding stops, call your doctor to discuss what happened. If the bleeding *doesn't* stop, go to the emergency room.

🦅 Sometimes while you are feeding the baby, particularly with a bottle, the baby could get milk into her windpipe. When that happens to adults, they gag and choke. Babies are far less able to manage that. They can't sit up or assist themselves to help clear their airway.

At that moment, the baby may look quite ill. She may be gagging, milk may be coming out of her nose, her face may turn red and then blue. As frightening as it appears, you must remind yourself that a baby cannot choke to death on milk. You must remain calm and act swiftly. Look in baby's mouth and make sure that she is not gagging because the nipple came off. If it did, pull it out. Turn her over, hit her hard across her back, blow in her face, and hold her upright. She should start to cry and be just fine in a matter of seconds. If she just doesn't quite seem right, call the doctor.

If these gagging incidents occur frequently, even if they are brief, report them to your pediatrician.

Calling Your Pediatrician

You will have an ongoing relationship with your baby's doctor. In addition to regular well-baby visits, you will probably need to call him or her periodically. The telephone can be a useful weapon in fighting childhood illness. Every doctor practices over the phone. With it we can diagnose and treat simple conditions. You should expect your doctor to be readily available to you. In fact, you may have chosen your pediatrician based on your perception of his or her accessibility.

The telephone can be a useful weapon in fighting childhood illness.

But here are some tips for getting the information you need:

- *Understand office etiquette.* It is important to know just how your doctor's office operates. In most offices, it's the receptionist who is at the front line, but she should not be expected to answer any health-related questions.

  The most common reason to call is to set up an appointment or to find out if you need one. In my office, anyone who requests an appointment gets one. If there is a question about whether you really need to bring your child in, talk directly to the doctor. Often I can make a suggestion or two and prevent an unnecessary visit.

- For obvious reasons, *don't engage the receptionist in small talk*, but you must be prepared to give pertinent information. Whenever you call—unless you are simply setting up an appointment—give your name and your child's name (today parents and children often go by different last names); your child's age; a sentence or two about the major symptoms or problem; and the phone number where you can be reached.

❧ *Find out if your pediatrician has a call-in hour.* A call-in hour is a specific time period set aside every day just to answer nonemergency questions. I don't have one anymore. I found that only a limited number of calls could get through, leaving a parent waiting until the next day for another opportunity.

❧ *Do your own "triage."* I instruct parents that when they call my office they should triage themselves. You can't expect the office receptionist to understand the world of difference between "relatively important," "sort of important" and "can wait until tomorrow."

If you say, "This is an emergency," or "This is urgent," that's the verbal equivalent of calling 9-1-1. Most doctors will expect to hear about an accident—head injury, broken bones, bleeding, an ingestion, a child not breathing right, very high fever (the definition of which is age-dependent).

❧ *Trust your instincts, always.* If you think something is wrong, you are probably right. Err on the side of caution. (When in doubt, it's worth checking out.) Call it parent's intuition, but no one is a better detective than you are at picking up the clues and cues—at reading the "flavor" of your child's mood or disposition.

❧ *When you call after office hours, it should be a matter of some importance.* If you call, you will invariably reach an answering service or an automated version of the same. Telephone operators have no training and often handle many clients at the same time. Try to leave a brief but specific message.

Some doctors leave instructions with their service to be called only for emergencies and they call in for groups of messages only every few hours. (If it's not urgent, ask the operator what time the doctor is likely to call in for his messages so you will know when to expect to hear from your doctor.)

🌢 When the doctor returns your call, you might want to *acknowledge the inconvenience or express your ambivalence.* ("I really didn't know if I should call you, but . . . ") Doctors are accustomed to reassuring new parents who are often not sure how to interpret and read their babies, who obviously can't speak for themselves.

I recently calmed a nursing mother who called at midnight because she noticed that she was rocking her baby underneath a smoke alarm that had a blinking red light. She couldn't wait until morning to be told that her baby was not being exposed to harmful radiation.

🌢 Before any phone visit is completed, *make sure you have all the information you need.* It is helpful to organize your thoughts and write down your questions before you call.

You can also call on a pediatrician for advice on a variety of topics at the drpaula.com Web site. Just visit this address:

http://forums.drpaula.com/doctor/

Coming Attractions

As your baby gets older, you will be taking her out more often and letting her interact with more people. At the same time, she will be slowly running out of your "borrowed" immunity and she will get more colds and run higher fevers. It's not unusual for a 4-month-old to have a cold and a fever of 102F/38.8C.

Babyproof!

Baby is mobile—and oral. At 4 months, your baby is increasingly mobile. She will begin to roll over and put all sorts of things in her mouth. You will need to be extra vigilant because your baby can get into more trouble. Clear the decks!

Check houseplants. Once babies can crawl across the rug, at 7 to 10 months, they can put plant leaves in their mouth. And they do. Call the doctor because she may have swallowed some resin from the plant.

It's a good idea to know the names of all the plants in your house. There is a big difference if she munched on a begonia, which is safe, or a dieffenbachia, which isn't. Get rid of all poisonous plants.

Poison-control telephone number. Always have the number for the poison control center handy. In most states it's **P*O*I*S*O*N*S.**

If you need to open her mouth fast, turn baby face down over your knee and squeeze where the jaw meets the ear, and her mouth will automatically open. Sweep her mouth with your finger.

Part IV

The Emerging Mother

11

The New Mother

After 3 months living with and lovingly caring for your baby, you are standing on a threshold, looking forward and backward at the same time. The paradox is that although the individual days may have seemed long (as one mom noted, "My days were longer because I rarely slept"), the weeks flew by.

It is both sweet and sad to say goodbye to your newborn. It seems that overnight, you went to bed with an infant and woke up with a baby. All of the "coming attractions" we have been describing are now arriving! At 3 months of age, your baby may sleep through the night, you may have decided to stop breastfeeding, and he is a much more active participant. In the next few months, he will roll over and sit up, and continue to gurgle, coo and "talk" to you.

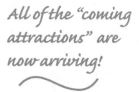

All of the "coming attractions" are now arriving!

The mothers of 3-month-olds usually get great satisfaction from seeing themselves in comparison to their "newborn" counterparts. On occasion, when a mother of a 3-month-old attends a group with mothers of newborns, she is treated like a wise, senior stateswoman. She is seen as having experience, confidence, competence. She's not as frazzled or worried about routines or daily care. At 3 months, mothers seem to have "systems"—whatever they are—in place. And there's that

> ### Celebrate!
>
> Three months is a naturally wonderful milestone for both you and your baby. Celebrate! Have an "unbirthday" party, take pictures and compare them with the pictures you took in the hospital right after the birth. You were probably bloated, pale. You may notice that in many of your early "baby" pictures, you have the baby "sitting" in front of you—as if you could hide behind a 7-pound infant. Revel in the changes that have occurred, and enjoy!

incredible feeling when it all begins to work out. For one mom, that happened when Joey started sleeping through the night regularly and his dad began giving him the 6:30 A.M. feeding. That meant she had the luxury of 8 hours of uninterrupted sleep.

Having workable systems in place doesn't mean there aren't still rough edges. As one mother put it, "I'm not quite the mom I pictured. I'm not living out the fantasies I had when I was pregnant. I envisioned putting Max into a Snugli and taking him everywhere I wanted to go. It didn't work out that way." Some of that disappointment has time to bubble up to the surface, now that you are not so "possessed" by exhaustion. (It's always helpful to talk about these feelings with other mothers who have been there.)

The New (Physical) Mother

You are not only stronger than when you first gave birth, but also you are less fragile mentally as well. (The mother-muddle fog should have lifted. As one mom joked, "When Jamie was a newborn, I had trouble addressing the thank-you notes. Sometimes I couldn't remember the towns people lived in.") Even to a casual observer, there is a noticeable difference. Often the mothers of 3-month-olds will come bouncing into my office wearing eye makeup for the first time or maybe a new hairstyle. You are probably now dressing almost as well as your

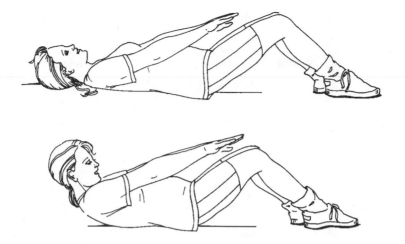

Modified sit-ups are a good way to regain your abdominal strength and tone. Keep your knees bent and the small of your back firmly pressed into the floor.

baby! You are no longer afraid to take the time to do more for yourself. You are gradually becoming a "renewed" mother.

There are physical changes *inside* as well, many triggered by your hormones.

- **Fat.** There is a type of fat, called *brown fat*, which is produced for the purposes of pregnancy. At 3 months, this fat begins to disappear, whether or not you are actively trying to lose weight. (You could say your "baby" fat begins to melt away!) This occurrence is linked to the changes in the percentages of your estrogen and progesterone levels, which settle by about three months.

- **Muscles.** During pregnancy, your abdominal muscles lengthened to accommodate your growing uterus. Now these same muscles shorten. Unfortunately, the other muscles that stretched at the same time don't magically shrink and you have to do the work by toning. (See illustration above.)

- **Breasts.** If you are still breastfeeding, your breasts will no longer appear swollen. The ducts have expanded enough so that you almost never have problems with engorgement.

You may even feel that your breasts look "empty"—but you *are* making milk.

- **Skin.** Dermatologists will tell you that most skin conditions will disappear at the end of 3 months whether or not you treat them. The warts, moles, patchy skin that suddenly appeared in pregnancy should all be gone. (Nature's "acne cleanser," so to speak, kicks in to clear up hormonally triggered blemishes.)

- **Hair.** Hair loss has slowed and the texture should be back to what it used to be.

By 3 months, your body has undone most of what pregnancy did. You are recovered enough to get back to your prenatal state. That's why 3 months is the time when you can "naturally" get pregnant again. In societies that don't look to regulate birth, babies are often spaced 12 to 14 months apart.

Reaching Out: Evolution

You have nurtured yourself and your newborn into a new state. As your 3-month-old changes physiologically and neurologically, she starts to look outward—to the world. She will try to sit up by arching her back. It's similar to the way you tentatively began to flex your muscles in order to rejoin the "real" world. You have both emerged from a cocoon you *needed* to be in. Now you are practically a butterfly and yes, you will have to test your wings before you can fly back to all of your previous relationships.

Back to Sex

In my new-mothers' groups, one question comes up over and over: "Am I ever going to have sex again?" The general refrain is one of exhaustion: "I'm just so tired." "Who has the energy?" "I don't want to waste my precious little time in bed having sex." The women admit to having thoughts as varied as: "Will it hurt?" "Will it feel the same?" "Will the baby wake up?" "Will I leak milk?" and "I'd rather spend the free time having coffee with a friend."

In a recent group, a mother had just gone for her own 1-month doctor's appointment. This is supposedly when she would get the green light to resume sexual relations. Her doctor asked her husband to wait outside and said, "You know your body is 'ready'." The woman asked the doctor not to bring the subject up in front of her husband. Later she hedged and told her husband, "Well, the doctor said I'll be ready in a few weeks."

> *The sex drive does return, but it rarely "gallops" at the same speed as before.*

This woman's story struck a responsive cord that resonated throughout the room. As another woman said, "All those magazine articles say that sex is a barometer of a normal marriage. If we don't have sex yet, does that mean we have an abnormal marriage?" Another woman burst out crying and confessed, "I don't think we are ever going to have sex again. I need to know, what's the longest time any normal couple has gone without sex?" She was panicked: "We'll never do it again, and my husband will find another woman." Even though she was not interested in sex, she thought she had better be.

I've surveyed several new mothers' groups and almost no one in my groups is having sex more frequently than once or twice in the first three months. The sex drive does return, but it rarely "gallops" at the same speed as before. (These same women describe very active romantic sex lives before the baby. As one woman said wryly, "We used to do it on the piano, on the couch, on the floor in the kitchen. Now we don't even do it on the bed.")

Tips

🔊 *Be comfortable with the fact that almost all new parents have to rediscover their sexual roles.* As new mother Susannah lamented on the television show *Thirtysomething*, "Gary and I used to have sex. Now we have . . . Emma."

Right after the baby is born, you will be fighting off the combined effects of fatigue and plummeting hormones. You can't go back to the sexual way you were and certainly not overnight. I suggest to women that I wouldn't be surprised if your partner isn't really eager for sex just yet either. Maybe there's something hormonally protective about this. Remember, you probably don't want to get pregnant again now. Your body is still depleted. (Babies who are born soon after a previous pregnancy are usually smaller and have the potential for a variety of related problems.)

🌢 *Seduce your partner only when and if you want to.* When you are ready for sex you could choose a date and not tell him in advance. Surprise him. You have the luxury of psyching yourself up all day, and if you change your mind, he won't be disappointed. (One woman who was not feeling totally comfortable with her body, bought Day-Glo condoms so they could make love in the dark.) Often not resuming sex is simply a result of logistics. You may have to schedule close encounters of the sexual kind.

🌢 *You must be clear about who the couple is in the relationship.* I talked to one mother about trying to recapture some of the romance and she said she felt like she would be cheating on the baby. Yes, she has a "lover" of sorts, but he's 6 weeks old and wears a diaper.

It's normal to feel that your baby is a new love.

It is, in fact, normal to feel that your baby is a new love. It's not a perversion. You can feel pleasure, even arousal while lying down and cuddling with your baby, or during breastfeeding. Your relationship with your baby does encroach on parts of you that were once reserved for your husband. It's helpful and healing to realize how universal these feelings are. They won't last forever.

Back to Being a Wife

The period right after birth is when the creation of a relationship with your baby is all-consuming. This is predictable and natural. Some cave woman first figured it out, and that's the way it's always been. This intense bonding is for the protection of babies. Call it Mother Nature herself rocking the cradle.

Adapting to New Roles

The overwhelming majority of couples choose to become parents, and they don't consciously choose to damage their relationship in the process. If anything, it's the love you shared that propelled you to want to have a baby in the first place. What many couples don't realize is that babies often act like little earthquakes, rocking the marital boat and causing aftershocks that take time to subside. Most parents have no idea how much their lives are going to change and they really are in shock. When a relationship consists of just two people, they usually have the time to be sensitive to each other's needs. But add a child to that equation and the attention gets diverted. Babies cry. Husbands usually don't, but that doesn't mean they don't still have needs as well.

> Babies often act like little earthquakes, rocking the marital boat and causing aftershocks that take time to subside.

The ties that bind couples together can sometimes be pried loose by little babies' fingers. There *are* couples who do unravel after the birth of a baby, but it's rarely because there is not enough sex. It's often because there was little commitment between them from the start. Also, many new mothers harbor deep resentment at new fathers who do almost nothing to help around the house. As one mom reported: "Before the baby, we shared chores. Now he says, 'You're home all day. You can do it all.'"

Without ever consciously asking, "Who comes first?" some mothers treat their marriage as if the answer is "The baby." Husbands come in a distant third in a contest they didn't know they had entered. Their jealousy may be overt ("I want to hug you and all you want to do is cuddle with the baby") or covert ("Gee, honey, it doesn't look like you really need me around, so I'll go out with the guys again").

While the child is an infant, no one should be asking, "Who comes first?" Babies do. But there comes a point when the bonding has a directional pitch. When the baby is about 3 to 6

The Princess and the Bea

There's a fine line to be walked between your relationship with your partner and your relationship with your baby. I like to talk in my mothers' groups about what I've come to call *The Story of the Princess and the Bea*. It's the story of the part-time working mom and full-time princess who jolted parents worldwide when she left her 6-week-old infant daughter to join her Prince for 6 weeks.

While most of us commoners treat our first-born like royalty, Sarah Ferguson, the Duchess of York, seemed to treat real-life princess Beatrice rather "commonly." To answer her many critics, Fergie pleaded her case via Barbara Walters and American telly. As the princess explained, "After nine months of looking enormous and my poor husband had to look at me, it was his turn." The "poor husband" didn't have too many supporters in his courtyard. (Of course we know now that this story didn't turn out "happily ever after" anyway!)

While making sure your husband knows he's important is perfectly acceptable, leaving a 6-week-old baby for 6 weeks generally receives the equivalent of thumbs down. Six weeks is just too early to decide your husband needs an exclusive turn.

months old, the pitch should start to be away from the child. Many mothers start to feel a desire to reestablish their relationship with their husbands. The natural course is to yearn for the person with whom you made the baby in the first place.

Find Time Together

But it is important not to turn away from your mate. Get reacquainted. There are circumstances pulling you apart, so you will have to work to pull yourself back together. Find time to be alone. Yes, go out for dinner. That may actually sound easier than it is. A mother in one of my new mothers'

It's time for partners to get reacquainted...

groups complained because her husband is insisting on taking her out for her birthday in a few weeks. She is already dripping with sweat and anxiety. It's not just the question of who will watch the baby, but that for the moment, the mother would really rather spend her time home with her new daughter. Another mother in the group counseled: "I know it's hard to believe, but in a few weeks, you are going to feel different."

By 3 months, it should feel less wrenching to be away from your baby. You and your husband may find yourselves literally worlds apart on this issue. He is ready to take a 3-week trip to Europe (without the baby) and you can't even manage a night out at the movies. Practice compromising now. Find a middle ground you can both live with.

Leaving Baby Home "Alone"— Baby-Sitters, Nannies and Others

Until their child is 2 or 3 months of age, many mothers really have no desire to be without their baby. You may actually feel like the baby is being ripped from you the first time you leave home without her.

You should be forcing yourself to go out (alone) for a walk, to get air without the baby attached to you, preferably by leaving the baby with your husband. Some new moms will leave the baby with a husband or mother, but that's about as far as the chain will stretch. And some moms have trouble leaving the baby with anyone at all. I have heard new fathers complain about their wives "little obsession." "She doesn't even trust me with my own baby." Or, "She goes out to do a few errands and then runs home early to check up on me."

Be careful what you do now or it could come back to haunt you later on.

Be careful what you do now or it could come back to haunt you later on. You don't want a child who can only be comforted by you. As one mother said, "It can choke you to always be the preferred parent."

Whether we talk about your going out to dinner with your husband, or even going back to work, the question is, "Whom do

I leave my baby with?" As one mother said recently, "I don't think I could ever trust anyone to take care of this baby. I love her so much, I can't imagine I would even have a good time. I would think that *she* wasn't having the best time. She can't possibly be as happy with someone else as she is with me." You have to let go of the notion that you can make this a perfectly comfortable world at all times for your baby.

You are slowly widening the "safety net" around your baby.

The real issue is not the practical considerations—how do you find a sitter or a nanny, or how do you interview—but how you feel about leaving your baby in the hands of a "stranger." Tell yourself you are really doing this for your baby. You are slowly widening the "safety net" around her. This is just another way you help your child emerge as a safe person and learn how to "fend" for herself, although a very little bit.

I can hear you saying, "But the sitter won't hold the baby the way I do." That's right. "She won't smell like me." That's true, too. Aren't you lucky that no one is you but *you*. But it's not a favor for your baby not to learn *other* people's smell and touch. You will be back! (And you and your baby will experience the pleasure of your return.) It is good for both you and your baby to be apart on occasion. There will be times when you need a baby-sitter, even if right now you feel you will never want one.

Letting Go

You have to learn to be okay with the notion that your baby can like someone else. One mother had to get the flu to "let go" of her baby Jenny. As she discovered, "I saw that she liked everyone—the baby-sitter, the housekeeper, my sister, everyone who came in to help out." For the moment Jenny is Miss Congeniality.

When you do use a baby-sitter, you can make the transition easier by leaving a T-shirt, nightgown or any article of clothing that does, in fact, smell like you. You should also stay at home for a while with the baby-sitter the first few times.

Let the "stranger" hold the baby, with baby facing toward you, while she gradually gets to know the new smells and sounds and then slowly let the sitter turn the baby to face her. And always trust your instincts. If you think the baby really doesn't like a baby-sitter, find another one.

> I've got some great tips for would-be baby-sitters on the drpaula.com Web site. Reviewing these tips with your new baby-sitter may give you additional peace of mind. Just visit:
>
> **http://www.drpaula.com/topics/babysit.html**

Back to Work

The question of when, and if, you should go back to work has no one right answer. No matter what choice you make you can't entirely "win."

The longest maternity leave most women can hope for is about 3 months. At that point women often have to go back to work or decide if they will take an unpaid leave and risk the possibility of never getting their job back.

By choice or by necessity, many women race right back to work. Though once a badge of honor for professional women, you rarely hear women bragging, "Oh I worked on Friday, gave birth on Saturday, and was back at work bright and early Monday." If you must get back to work, at least consider your options carefully.

In making the decision, the first question usually is: Do you have to go back to work? If it is not essential to return quickly to work for financial or other reasons, many more women are choosing to stay home than did previously. It's become more acceptable to see mothering as the vital, important and difficult "work" that it is. If you previously held a satisfying job, you may still have to grapple with the feeling that you are now not really "doing" anything. How untrue! One mother who was annoyed with her husband asking, "What do you do all day?" prepared a memo outlining exactly what she did! (Keep a diary and you may be astonished at just how many activities your day encompasses.)

The downside of staying home is that many women are still embarrassed to say that they don't "work." I tell mothers to answer the question for themselves this way: "Yes, I'm going back to work. I'm now working as a mother." Keep reminding yourself that you are very lucky to be able to have this opportunity. You are nurturing the future.

Many women go back to work because they have to.

Many women go back to work because they have to. We are a two-paycheck society by necessity. As both a worker and mother, you will struggle to find a balance. At home you will be thinking about work, and at work you will be daydreaming (or even "nightmaring") about your baby at home. You have one foot planted in each world, and you will be torn. It's almost easier to justify working if you *have* to work. You can tell yourself, "I do the minimum, I will stay the minimum. Then I'm out of here and with my child."

Some new moms suddenly find that work, as fulfilling as it is, doesn't have quite the same importance as it once did. I just heard the "confession" of a dentist, a single mother, who said, "Work was once my major source of gratification. I still like what I do, I'm good at it, but I do it now more for the money." The paycheck she picks up provides her with an environment she can enjoy with her daughter.

Many women go back to work because they love their jobs.

Many women go back to work because they love their jobs. Yes, they love their babies as well, but some women really need to get back to the "real" world, which for them is the world of work. Going back to work should always be viewed as a viable option, and I tell women not to feel guilty about their choice. It is definitely possible to be both a good mother and good worker.

Some women who really love their jobs are concerned about the economics of working. As one woman explained, "When I figure out all that it costs me to work, it hardly pays." That doesn't mean she shouldn't work. (A reasonable approach would be to "charge" half of the cost of "daycare" to your husband's paycheck instead of considering that your check should cover 100 percent.)

Working It Out: Working

New moms who are returning to the work force are filled with the anxiety of practicality: How do I go back? When? Who will watch my child? What if she needs me? How will I juggle roles? How do I convince the people at work that I can still be productive without "killing" myself in the process?

Make the transition back to work easier: If you know you are going to return to the work force, then don't cut off all communications between your professional and personal life. Stay in contact so that

You will have to make an effort on all fronts.

people know you are coming back. Check in with co-workers occasionally and ask to have reports and newsletters sent home. If it feels right, visit your office once with the baby—particularly if they made a big fuss before you left. You might want to visit one more time (without the baby) and check up on mail and paperwork. On your first day back, arrive early, as a businesswoman—not a mommy—although you will undoubtedly call home often. (And don't hang up too many baby pictures.)

If you have made the decision to go back to work, the one area where you don't compromise is childcare. You want to find someone who is as wonderful in as many ways as possible: warm, loving, competent. You do not scrimp or cut back on childcare. Period.

On the professional front: Expect less of yourself. You are still a team player, but you may not be able to always go the extra yard. Even if you truly love your work, you may not continue on exactly the same track you left. (And you may find that others have figuratively placed you on the infamous "mommy track.")

Work will not be the same, because you are not the same.

Work will not be the same, because *you* are not the same. Lay your cards out on the table now and there should be less hostility later. If you were known as the office workaholic, you will have to clearly state that you are no longer so "addicted." (Many women find that having a baby is an instant cure for workaholism!) Talk to your staff frankly and understand that delegating is an absolute must. Now when your boss comes in at 5:00 P.M. with a new project for you to do, you will just have to say, "I'll do it tomorrow." (If your sitter has to leave at 6:00 P.M., you have no choice but to go home, or you may find yourself sitter-less very quickly.)

> I like the following Web site for information
> about choosing childcare:
>
> **http://www.voiceofwomen.com/childcare.html**

After a few months of full-time work, you may want to go to your boss and bring up the subject of part-time work. Don't assume the answer will be "no." I tell my new mothers: "Let me plant a seed. Your company probably has no policy for taking you back on a part-time basis, but that doesn't mean you can't be the first."

Many women today are negotiating a variety of flexible time arrangements. It's not perfect, of course. As one part-time lawyer admitted, "Look, they don't give me the important, meaty cases, and I'm not going to be made partner, but the hours are flexible, it pays well, and gives me benefits. And it makes me really appreciate my son when I get home."

Breastfeeding and Work

It is possible to continue to nurse even after you return to the work force.

❧ You can *express breast milk* at work that will be fed to your child by the baby-sitter the next day. Go into the bathroom or close the office door, if you have the luxury of your own office. To save time, express milk with an electric or battery-operated breast pump. (Practice at home by expressing milk between feeds. Don't be concerned if you don't express much milk at first. The more often you pump, the better the flow.) You will need a place to store the milk. If you refrigerate it, you can use it for up to 48 hours. Bring a coolpack to work to carry home the milk. (Don't put the milk in a freezer at work, because it will defrost on the way home and cannot be refrozen.)

❧ You can choose not to express milk at work and still *continue to nurse at home*. At work, again, find a bathroom and squirt off just enough milk to relieve the tenderness and pressure caused by the buildup of milk. *Don't* pump or you will just stimulate production of more breast milk. If you can, put cool compresses or ice packs on your breasts. It should take about a week for your body to figure out you are not "using" your breasts between the hours of 9 and 5. When you do get home, your baby will cry when hungry, and your milk should flow once again. Many mothers only nurse from about 6 in the evening to 8 in the morning. The baby may even adapt to your shift and only need an additional 1 to 3 bottles during the day. (This method isn't foolproof! Some women come home from work tired and anxious and do not produce enough milk. I suggest these moms pump at work.)

❧ If you are planning to breastfeed, then *continue to drink a lot of liquid and bring breast pads to work* for those times when you leak. It's also important to make sure you have introduced formula to your baby at about 1 month. It can be harrowing if you try to introduce formula after 3 months. Many babies reject it. (Even if you express breast milk at the office, you still need to leave a few backup bottles of formula, because you may not have pumped quite enough.) At home, instruct your sitter initially to feed the baby in her arms holding a T-shirt or nightgown that you have worn. (This position doesn't always work, because some babies more than 3 months of age don't like to be "intimately" fed by someone else. In this case, have the sitter put baby in an infant seat and then feed your baby the bottle.)

This syringe style breast pump is one of the many types now available. Start with a simple one and be patient with yourself. The more often you pump the more you'll produce.

Visit the breastfeeding forum at the drpaula.com Web site to ask questions and receive support from other women who want to continue to breastfeed their baby after returning to work:

http://breastfeeding.drpaula.com/topics/optimizing.html

On the home front . . . you are now part of the juggling generation. The trick is to see how many roles you can keep in the air at once without them all crashing down around you. Some simple advice:

- Get great help.
- Balance the load with your mate.
- Ease into the next working day by getting ready the night before.
- Have a backup "pinch sitter" in place.

It's been noted that the average working mother comes home to what has been called "the second shift"—cleaning, cooking, caring for the children. Decide early on that you can't be too concerned with the concept of "quality" time. How many parents come home after a full day's work and have any type of time for their children or—even less likely—for themselves? Yet they carry the additional burden of thinking that when they are home, the time with their children has to be the so-called "quality time." That can lead to what I call "frantic parenting."

"Gee, I only have one hour with my baby, I better cram all the quality of the week into it." Quality time simply means making the most of every experience you do share. Slow down and enjoy the time you have.

Never forget that happy mothers raise happier babies. If you are always the giver and never on the receiving end of tender-loving care, it can lead to depression and all sorts of self-abuse. I've seen many working women, particularly those who are in the "helping"  professions, who don't take adequate care of themselves. They are perpetually tired and never feel complete either as a mother, a worker or a woman. Women need to also give to themselves. (It's almost always the wife who pays the price for working when the psychological bill comes due.)

We all know at least 1 woman who does seem to "do it all." This superwoman transforms from perfect mom to worker effortlessly. She always looks terrific and even manages to make cookies and Halloween costumes from scratch. We tend to imagine this woman is very happy: possibly, but not probably. You don't know what the actual costs are, because no one has manufactured a magic pill that replaces the need for sleep.

I counsel new mothers all the time: Don't look outward, look *inward.* Think of all that you have accomplished in 3 months and how far you and your baby have traveled since your journey began with your baby's first cry. You are, in fact, a pretty super woman already.

Epilogue

The Future

Six months ago you met a little stranger. You may have loved her on sight, but you didn't know her. Now you do. As one mother of a 4-month-old said recently, "I can't even picture life without *this* face." These first months are a contained amount of time during which you are learning to become the mother you will be.

Although we've covered all the basics of baby care in this book, you are still going to make mistakes. Even with information, it's normal to worry. We need to acknowledge just how anxiety-producing raising a baby can be.

Raising babies is not an exact science.

A mother recently rushed into my office because she was boiling bottles for 5 minutes and seemed to remember my saying something about "nipples breaking down." "Oh no," she said, "Have I hurt my baby?" Then she pulled the nipple out of her bag and it was silicone, not polyvinyl. I said, "I don't care how long you boil silicone nipples. You sure don't have to, but they don't break down." Before I reassured her, there was palpable anxiety in the room. There will be many such "overboiling" occasions in parenting. And many more times when we can learn from each other.

It was from a parent that I relearned how to easily open the eyes of a baby. Early in my career I asked a mother to put eye drops in her baby's eyes and I asked, "How did you manage to pry her eyes open?" She said, "I discovered if I put my finger in

201

her mouth, her eyes opened wide." From that moment on, I shared that with all the other mothers in my practice. Mothers are wonderful students and teachers rolled into one.

Raising babies is not an exact science. You can't cultivate perfect babies the way you can grow prizewinning tomatoes. It's worth repeating that you will learn by trial and lots of error. It's important that you don't ever judge yourself too harshly.

In one of my new-mothers' groups, a mother told of her husband, who recently read a study suggesting that by 6 months, a baby has learned all the sounds of his language. The father misinterpreted that to mean that babies learn all language by 6 months, and so he now reads to his son from the dictionary every night. All the other mothers in the room laughed.

Future Fearing

I watched once during a routine visit as a new mother continuously moved her daughters' fingers out of her mouth. Every time her daughter sucked on her fingers, mom removed them. I finally asked, "What worries you about that?" She replied, "I'm worried that she'll have an overbite." I sensed there was more. Finally she responded, "I knew a young girl who always sucked on her fingers and she grew up to be clingy and whiny."

Another mom called with this worry: "My mother says I will psychologically damage my 3-week-old son if I continue to kiss him on his lips." I call this *future fearing*— the mistaken belief that if a mother doesn't do the right thing now for her infant, or makes a mistake, there will be a wrong and irreversible outcome later on.

We cannot predict the future, and it is not usually the things we worry about that come to pass. We may as well calm down and "smell the roses."

Our first inclination was to dismiss this as ridiculous. On further thought, it was suggested that perhaps his dictionary reading was a male version of reading nursery rhymes and singing lullabies. There is a serious side to all of this. As the mother observed, "He is very upset if he misses a day." And the mother also admitted to having similar feelings: "I'm worried that if I don't provide the right atmosphere for him, he'll be bored as a child and boring as an adult." What a burden to put on the shoulders of parents! What many parents can't quite say out loud, they say to themselves: "If I don't do the right thing now, my child will be a permanently messed-up human being." Parents feel a lot of pressure.

I always try to remove those future fears. You really have to stop believing that any one thing you do now will have far-reaching ramifications later on.

The first 6 months are the launching pad that should propel you happily into the future. Remember when you came home from the hospital and said, "What do I do now?" The answer is, enjoy your baby—your new, little, very best friend!

Index

A

accidents, household
  baby's head getting banged, 173-174
  bleeding from, 174
  dropping baby, 173-174
  gagging on milk, 174-175
adoption, Web site, 40
advice, child rearing. *See* child-rearing advice
afterbirth (placenta), following delivery, 4, 25
aftercare for new mothers. *See* hygiene and aftercare
alcohol, drinking
  and breastfeeding baby, 81
  having occasional glass of wine, 69
allergic reactions to formula, baby having, 171
  Web site, 172
alone, new mothers often feeling in the recovery room, 26-27
Apgar score (test done on newborns), 5-6

B

babies. *See also* newborns
  development of
    at 2 weeks, 162
    at 6 weeks, 165
    at 2 to 3 months, 165
    at 3 months, 145, 152, 160, 181-182
    at 4 months, 178
  finding comfort in inanimate objects, 126
  having growth spurts, 96
  new mothers facing future fears, 201-203
  when no longer considered newborn, 134
"baby blues," 59-60, 63, 71. *See also* postpartum depression
baby massage, 156-158, 160
  for head after bath, 132
baby monitors, why not recommended, 119
babyproofing home, 178
baby-sitters
  new mothers allowing someone to watch newborn, 191
  Web site, 191

bald, most babies born, 12
bathroom, new mothers and
  bowel movement, first, 26, 34, 36
  urination, first time, 34
baths, 128-132
  baby bathtub, using a, 130
  baby getting used to, tips for, 128-129
  baby's first, 20-21
  boys versus girls, tips for cleaning, 132
  cotton balls, avoiding use of, 131
  head of baby should never be submerged, 131
  how often. 128
  powders and talc, avoiding use of, 131
  soap, type to use, 130
  sponges, using baby-sized, 130
  time of day for, 128
  toys in bathtub, 130
beach, taking baby to the, 147
bedding, 109-110
  for first 6 to 8 weeks, 39
bedroom for baby
  equipment
    bassinet, 109
    bedding, 109-110
    blankets, 110
    crib, 110
    mattress, 109
    pillows, caution regarding, 110
bedtime. *See also* sleep
  developing a ritual for newborn, 114-115
  letting baby know it's time for, 111
bilirubin level, and jaundice, 22, 23
birth certificate for newborn, 40
birth control, myth that breastfeeding will prevent pregnancy, 90
birth of baby. *See* labor and delivery
birth weight, 8
birthmarks on newborns
  only temporary, 7, 11-12
  red marks (nevus flameus) on base of neck, 11-12
bladder control, new mothers regaining following birth, 64
bonding with newborn, 5, 30-31
  father, 103

Paula Elbirt, M.D., went from treating scores of children in her Park Avenue office to advising the parents of thousands of children all over the world. Dr. Elbirt, who returned call after call from worried parents every day after office hours, says her practice was the inspiration for drpaula.com, the pediatric web site she founded with her husband in 1997. The site is the only one to have a doctor answer every question posted by parents about their children's health. It receives more than 3 million hits each month and registers 600 new users a week.

Dr. Elbirt opened her pediatric practice in 1983. She teaches at Mount Sinai/NYU Medical Center and Lenox Hill Hospital in New York City, where she holds appointments as Assistant Clinical Professor of Pediatrics. Dr. Elbirt was recently appointed Director of Primary Care Education in the Department of Pediatrics at The Brooklyn Hospital Center, an affiliate of Presbyterian/New York Cornell Medical Center.

Dr. Elbirt has contributed articles to many consumer publications, including *Parents, Glamour* and *Healthy Kids,* as well as a teen guide on adolescent issues. She also appears as a pediatric consultant on national television.